DIALOGUE

POETRY BY
VINCENT SPINA

THE POET'S PRESS
PITTSBURGH, PA

Copyright 2015 by Vincent Spina
All Rights Reserved
Second Printing, 2017

The following poems first appeared in magazines:
"Text Messages" in *Arsenic Lobster;*
"Three Sentences" and "Riso Amaro"
in *Voices de la luna;*
"La Castella — Crotone Province"
in *Making Connections;*
"Castel Dell'Ovo — Bay of Naples"
in *The Bridge.*

THE POET'S PRESS
2209 Murray Avenue #3
Pittsburgh, PA 15217
www.poetspress.org
This is the 212th book from The Poet's Press

ISBN 0-922558-79-5

CONTENTS

BOTTLE
    Bottle   9
    Morning   10
    Anolis Lizard   11
    East End   12
    Fossil Shark Tooth   14

DIALOGUE
    Text Messages   17
    A Possible Title   19
    Three Sentences   22
    County Fair   25
    Sycamores in Winter   28
    Dialogue   31

WINTERS IN PARIS
    Winters in Paris   51
    Knots   53
    Long Name   55
    Rejoice, Lamb   57
    Falling   58

NEW YORK IN AUTUMN
    New York in Autumn   61
    Aquarelle   62
    Gloss on a Gloss   63
    You Saw the End   65
    Saturdays   66

ROCCA DI NETO — STONE ON THE RIVER
    You Old Dog You   71
    Sistine Chapel   73
    Castel Dell'Ovo — Bay of Naples   75
    Rocca di Neto: Stone on the River   77
    La Castella — Crotone Province   79
    Riso Amaro   80
    Arriving at Pompeii   82

ABOUT THE POEMS   85
ABOUT THE POET   87
ABOUT THIS BOOK   88

For Mary Spina

BOTTLE

BOTTLE

The immeasurable morning was back again;
the greater and lesser catastrophe, leaving
its wake of pain, now slept
in the kitchen alcove waiting for day
to give it a proper sendoff,
that we might survive again
having captured a small wave of time
and made it safe in a bottle. With this
and because you are a frequent walker
through cemeteries where stone epitaphs
speak a language of flowers, I text you now:
One night by midnight
the quieting moon had risen across
the dream-mined prairie. All the loving
and decorative corpses — she among them —
had settled into memory. Living
in this less pure space, swallowed within
the unbreathing, unspeaking white eternal,
we spoke for a little while of
Sunday brunches: movies ending
in cliches, simple enough
for all to understand. Rivers,
for instance. Don't forget
how we all loved rivers.

MORNING

Mmm   the silence sounds good.
All the right chords are lined up; the snow
has risen from the ground in all
the right places while small intimacies
of sun turn bare patches green and make
them forget. We are all parts-and-parcels
involved in it — the way the right twists in
the fiber define a cord, and the knots in
the fiber weave us our place. We were simply
returning from the corner grocery store
— the scents of cheese, ocean, and rare olives
heavy around us. One of us found
a pen, or something wrapped carefully
and abandoned   was how it started:
the mesh reentered, the chance
to be restrung in our favorite twine
and colors. You, who never say your name
anymore, could stitch a million things if
only someone listened. Was it I who did?
I heard water running over leaves
and into snow. It was like the first
advance of the light around us: the world about us, still
and amber

ANOLIS LIZARD

The tiny brains of brown and green anoles,
bobbing with ecstasy and rage, know
something they are too tiny to know;
though, yes, it is already much late
in the day, persistence flies a red flag
not caring what dewlap is arthritic. And, yes,
it is "oh-so" confusing: this nebula
of woven palmettos, hibiscus and beach
grape shrubs begging the question of how
you fit … like the mockingbird's song
you are singing now. No joy, no grief
or meditated contemplation, comes close to,
much less matches, the simple act of living.
You know the rest … which was always the meaning
behind your morning shave in the mocking glass mirror.
The stink of car horns from a nearby highway
mixes with offshore breezes, mockingbird flight,
the anole's outrageous claim to his leaf
on a twig.

EAST END

Assortment of periwinkles, slipper
and corrugated scallop shells in magentas,
the varied lives of pinks and creams,
scattered among pebbles bled
from the sides of maternal mountains ...
pincers of a small spider crab
washed into close proximity
by the last full-moon tide as if
the body that once joined them were
still there.   One more
palm at the end of mind, song
without human meaning. Yet the question
of observer and observed winds through
the morning like an unrequited sea-worm
through ocean bottom ... how one may
alter the other: principle of uncertainty,
a change of place to potential.
I, for one, am touched: how the shore
is an endless graveyard of mollusk
and crustacean shells, and ground
of endless restoration.
One mile east from where I stand
Long Island ends its edgy New York
dialogue with self on a beach
of foam and detritus,

perhaps to be picked up once more
on any day like today, brimming
with quick overtures and vast
and shoreless endings ... deeply,
mightily, though in a different language,
ancestral yet still ours:
a vocabulary of waves,
syntax of empty shells,
the luster of sea-washed pebbles.

FOSSIL SHARK TOOTH

Waves
and the countless breath of tides:
the cutting edge is gone. Serration
relaxes into a smooth, continuous surface
I rub to please the tip of my finger
as boys run their surf boards
into the surf, or, waist deep in the tepid,
gulf water, climb onto each other's shoulders
like wrestlers or lovers.
See.
Petrifaction changes the simple
innocence of the carnivore into something
not so simple: the white kill, into shades
of brown and ocher
that shine in the fading sun.
Much like the old need for defense
and the need to penetrate the defense of others
soften into
more lasting and complex longings,
disperse
into a memory someone might find
in the sand.
The impression those lovers,
who now pick up their blanket to leave,
have left in the sand.

DIALOGUE

TEXT MESSAGES

I
Listen.
The message on the screen is for you.
My hope is that you take
it over, plan something in the margin
or in the interim to make
it yours. Look.
The many texts you have sent
stand silent, glyphed black to rock
walls painted in reds and yellows.
Judas trees bleed where once
an alga ocean slept
                       — distance
and the braying of a desert burro content
to graze on what the landscape wills her.

II
Here mementoes twist about your knees
like the vines of a strangler fig
around the limbs of its victim tree.
Blue green algae drape the sofa. Moss
steals from the basement into your bones.
Then, the itinerant pang of sorrow
rolls back the forest lianas as an echo
emerges from the cleansed desert stones
— whose or for what the message doesn't say;
it is only a dream, these are only poems.

III
A recent crisis has arisen in the sandwich
you have swallowed for lunch. It sticks somewhere
in the blueprint you are unrolling.
A poem in winter hangs like a cylinder
from a tree. From a basement window
I see you grey through bands of drifting snow,
glossing the white screen,
reading me into the line.

A POSSIBLE TITLE

These uncontrollable coughing fits begin somewhere
in the right cerebral hemisphere and continue
radiating outward until it is no use pretending
you are awake. The old folks used to call it rheumatism
but every Saturday they'd still don their Legion caps
and vote Republican,
and having lost
a watch or diamond encrusted pearl
you are searching in a village common — it could be
Boston Common. It is early Spring Time.
We spend summers by the coast,
winters further inland. Boston has no law
prohibiting interfaith marriages — it wasn't
Boston yet, we've lost the name. For now all unions
will be legal though future ghosts shall
refrain from strong spirits and women
of stronger spirit. Back then there was
little pork to eat, or beer to drink, nor did we watch
much television. Later, sheep came to graze
in the meadow and someone
was tolling a bell. It is the dinner bell calling you home.
Could it be this long to healthier bones
and sounder moral fiber? The village lass
would laugh were she only allowed to take time
from her busy schedule of stitching and unstitching.

Sheep are on everybody's mind these days, and how many bells
till the circus rides are all packed into the tent
and us with them. So, we have a bell, we feel comfortable
living in a shadow, there is a cat, and so it fell
to the circus side show and the village priest to bless
the gooey spillage when the last black mussel
and juicy oyster were extracted from the bay.
Some of his best friends knew and the village
blacksmith knew something they weren't telling,
yet despite the dung and bodies heaped
on the cowpath the cowpath grew. They were free
to give full rein to their passions and secreted inhibitions:
The well-manured fields were a good thing,
the rocky ledge where the land ends and the ocean begins.

There were the merry men, the national
monument to the undead soldier, the fox and
turkey trots, the Lindy Hops, the Counter Reformation,
Reconstruction and Rosy, The Burlesque Queen.
Waves and more waves,
generous in their hunger for more visitors,
more tourists and more shore.
How many times bleeding, by then,
had he gone to her window searching for that woman-girl
only to hear her father lament like one more wave
against the beaten shore: "My Son, I am no longer
myself nor is my home my home. How many times
had she waited, how many times was she lost
— encrusted pearl, on the village common green?"

Where to go they prayed as each one's hands searched
for the other's buttocks and thighs. Bridges to the floating
kingdom, church picnics, the indecent three leg races
fathers coveting their wives reincarnated
in their daughters. For this we traveled these many
miles, for this we come together
— the local parish priest foretold —
for this and these bites of cheese
melting in the shadow …
and church bells,
clappers gone missing.

THREE SENTENCES

One:
It's what remains when the autopsy ends
but the results are inconclusive,
a space in the mind
when the lyrics and melody are gone,
like the movement that last streamlet of water,
sinking through the sand, leaves after the wave
has washed back
— the rhythm a dream plants
in your mind, or a poem ... waiting
for the words to return.

Two:
It happens in stages, gradually, like a sycamore,
the pattern of its white branchings
inscribed already into its genome,
now planted against a gray, late winter hillock
weeks before leaves
may appear,
the way a coast anticipates the next high tide, syncopated
as is the nature of things, just one hour later
than yesterday
as you dream it into a tide-flat waiting
to be filled ... replete
with red knots and sandpipers eluding the waves
as they wash in following the wave path out,
terns diving on a chance notion as black-
back seagulls watch from rotten mooring posts
— sort of like God, though not in the once
popular sense of a mid-day *auto-da-fé*
or a city left in ashes as ram horns
echo triumph in the distance

but in the hollow
sense of things or a god
that need not be filled since addition
tends to diminish the issue, which is
the silence between the end of your last dream of night
and the radio's "blast from the past"
the silence after distant thunder
or after the unexpected cough
from deep in your throat you take the next
ten minutes to worry about,
which is only one knot
in a string of knots you were issued
long ago though you can't know exactly when
by someone though you don't remember exactly whom,
— each knot like a vindictive bee sting
though you have stolen no honey nor stepped
barefoot on any bee, and you say as
to the silence that, yes, this is
exactly where you wished to be, and, yes,
theirs is a well of words which
may deepen this silence, weaving it into patterns
of erotic velvets, tropical and night dew,
and without thinking there comes the next wave
in the rhythm

— a child stumbling to
the top of a hummock, somewhere among
the first hundred steps his life has taken and raises
his arms to embrace the morning empty air,
and just when you think you
have it, you don't for the child is
carried away.

Three:
All around, plovers and terns
have settled down along the pebbly beaches,
one there, one here, dozing, or looking about, or
grooming the barbs of a feather back into place,
and you remember they once used those quills
to write a letter or a postcard you may wish
to place in the mail this afternoon
and are now searching your pockets
for an address.

COUNTY FAIR

On the floor of a fossil sea
it is a sultry evening in late August.
The judges have met and made their decisions.
Red, blue and gold ribbons hang above
the stalls of Guernsey cows with the most nutritious milk
and the stall of the finest sloe-eyed Jersey heifer,
and merino ram with softest fleece. A first place
jungle Banty crows in dazzlement of gas lights, town
and country folk, come to admire him, as well as each other.
A herd of lumbering Leedsichthys float in, hungry
for the plums of pink plankton radiating
in swirls above the midway grills where sweaty hot dogs
roast alongside sizzling burgers and sausages
smothered in onions and peppers. Nearby, the aroma
of funnel cakes. The ubiquitous presence of pizza.
Always pizza.
A lone trilobite scuttles along the perimeters, seeking
comfort among the horseshoe crabs, who,
early in the season, spawned along this Appalachian ridge,
and now seek only nourishment and rest.
She is the last of her kind.
But what force binds words to word to express
the electromagnetic fields of young girls who cluster
in threes and fours, revealing/concealing the newly found
secrets of hips and breasts, whose eyes meet and avoid
the gaze of young boys clustered in threes and fours
lighting their cigarettes with the fallen embers
of a distant volcano? Words fall apart. Syllables
float away like fireflies or tiny stars: tension wrapped
in calm ... the moment captured in amber.
A white county transport van parks nearby
a medium-sized gazebo, a cargo
of the elderly descends from the sliding door

like drops of colored water,
wanting and not wanting to stay
or be assumed into a vast and unknown sea.
They each take a seat under the gazebo as
volunteer wives of the local Knights of Columbus
serve them the regional specialty of chicken
and dumplings. "We can't recall,"
they whisper, "who was the banker
among us or an ammonite,
who fought in a civil war, or
was a refugee hidden in a ship's galley,
or fossil displayed in a museum
or on a shelf in a jewelry store."
Tomorrow will be the demolition derby,
tonight grey doo-woppers with silver
comb-overs wonder, "Who Wrote the Book
of Love?"
A leopard tamer in leopard leotards
prepares her leopard act ... hardest of the big
cats to train. She spiels to an audience —
young and old — as wild leopards
filament gills swim in every ocean dingle
and coral shelf, dreaming life and fear into
relentless leather-backed archelons and
emerald and ruby protostegas, their distant cousins.

For now
the public is pleased
— hunger, suspended, the lure of future
and the pull of past are suspended. We have become
a people, neither hollow nor full ...
our heads, only heads, as we watch a school
of incoming plesiosaurs, enormous necks
and minute heads, breaching the surface
in search of horizon we may live in more
than just in a dream of ourselves — time
between the last act and the next.
"A hundred times," the silver voices sing,
"they've told me you were leaving." A hundred times
we sit before this simple meal. In a next time around
perhaps there will be cities. Taxies like
yellow blood cells will bring nourishment and oxygen
to ever more labyrinthine interiors, but here
on the floor of a shallow vanished sea, the cupboard
and closets are bare, save the many things
we have no use for anymore. Vast creatures
float by nudging us like kittens
wishing to be petted. They pet us in return.
Sometimes we weep and call out
like an echo calling out and weeping love
and compassion back to us,
but mostly we forget.

SYCAMORES IN WINTER

I
If there were a long name for things
— the one starting as the thing starts
and continues through memory and past
to where memory itself is lost   if so
what would the long name of a lone
sycamore in winter be?   "Grey Ghost
of the forest," maybe, "Placed
on the bank of a river biding time
under cracked blankets of ice   Two Trunks
that emerge from a single stump
— Sister and Brother   Two Lovers   Branches
not like other trees'   They Twist
out to cross the river like a snake's tongue
turned to ice and mist   Patches of old bark
clinging to the sides like a Message
to be read, turned once again to a Bass Line
of a musical score   carried within the river
through underground channels of cities
to a waiting bay in late winter,
early spring."

II
Two centuries prior, fourteen
of the last Susquehannock people
were beaten to death by a mob of whites
in the jailhouse of Conestoga Town. *Susquehannock*
is what the Delaware called them, an Algonquian word
meaning "people of the muddy river."
We don't know what they called themselves
or the river. The long names are gone.
Their language is lost.
Among random footnotes, however, history
records they were noted for their courage,
their "esprit de corps" having fended off encroaching
Senecas and Onondagas from the West and North
— their cousins and bitter enemies —
Shawnees and Delawares from the East and South
dispossessed by invading English and Dutch.

III
Animus is the Latin word for "courage,"
"Life giving force," or "spirit"
— masculine singular.
Anima is the feminine meaning "soul."
In an outlier's fantasy script, say,
we could imagine a sycamore
has *animus* — a part of its long name:

"Pale glow that emerges from a grove
of white and red pines   Facing the river
in winter   Augur of spring frozen in time
suspending its breath   Illusion
among trees, whispering to themselves
or to those who listen:

IV
"In a birch canoe," the long name continues,
"I followed the river to where it enters a shallow
though nutritious bay   There were steel and concrete
cities at each turning   It was night
There was a woman asleep like a soul
to be wakened
In a dream — hers or mine — I wooed her
Through spring and summer we feasted
"on fresh oysters   wild bass   and blue claw crabs
In autumn we returned to the river
to wait out the snow and the ice
in a grove of red and white pines
— the tree of peace —
where we sing to each other
the long name of things   and ourselves
each to the other."

DIALOGUE

I
You can say it

But I don't think I ...

But you can say it. It's like confession
but this time it can't take you there.

Will anything?

Wait.   *Then what?*   Wait.

In Spain, they say it sounds like poetry: "Me suena a poesía." Meaning?

Meaning, *saccharine at best ... ultimately false; a line cast out*
  "across a crowded room" and the room swills of beer, scented florals
  and previously perfumed underwear.

Go on.

An expression is all. All over Madrid. Ask any suit about the economy,
  the economist, the theory of light, about the EU, or the Euro:
  "Es poesía, pura poesía." Poetry, pure poetry.

And history and science and the goblin that comes up to your car
  in a dream asking for a handout or your child or poetry itself?

"Pura poesía." Made for the moment. The house and home
  you sweep under the rug when the phone rings,
                                        the doorbell rings
  and it is the exterminator,
  bill collector, collector of old and forgotten debts,

*false steps, the endless flow of consequences or
it is precisely five o'clock of the afternoon,
"las cinco en punto de la tarde," when all things
come to a halt in Madrid: Lorcan dream in the dust
of a countless time.*

And the poplars that line the boulevards of Madrid
and other tourist destinations?

*Poplars, oaks, maples, magnolias; they take us to a here,
too close to other truths ("poesías") where we live
the undiscovered continent. Lost in history, lost in myth,
of blood, of fire and water, courage ... the saliva of despair;
the vast descent of wandering peoples, while others
ascend a mountain the taste of suicide.*

*In Texas poplars are "álamos"
Ask your average origin-unknown Texan.
He knows nothing. "Álamos" are myth
— what is included, what is left out.
He walks past an entrance, past
a Mexican gardener, spearing M&M wrappers,
pruning an odd bush, knowing nothing . . .
except a vague feeling crawling like a worm
down his back that a somewhere was here
once, and he wants it and doesn't know.
He sees or dreams of "poesía" all around
him: the Mexican picking up the M&M wrapper
he has dropped, the existence of the Mexican
himself, and worse; what is not "poesía"
(in the local tongue: bullshit), is the sightless
dragon eating all his values: Mexican and child.*

So does it end at the wall swinging an empty
flintlock in a raccoon skin cap
at the advancing forest of poplars?

I have no idea, no tengo idea.

Can you say it?

*It's rough, prefers it that way, a dim star
or any light you may only see from the corner
of the eye ... oblique essence. I haven't thought
in years ... my bones ... my bones following the scent
of sex down a street ... the perfect language, dead
on completion. I don't know if I am telling a story
of my bones or creating my bones themselves.*

But you will attempt it?

What choice is there?

Then?

*I am holding my two hands in front of my eyes,
turning them,
first: palms facing in, then, palms facing out
I want to be acquainted with them once again ...*

Much like Pablo Neruda, in the simple odes he wrote to his socks,
artichokes and
other things ... things
of this world ... white bed-sheets
on a pulley who wake you up one morning?

... and what they can do and what they cannot do.
the years have worn them down, the way an ocean may
wear a shore away, how the nails
shred and break
how they remain the default,
the condition of the shape
of all the instruments and tools
I will ever see or make. The third dimension
of your first real contact ... after sight, after smell ...
they are the feel.

Now form them into two guns,
the way we did as children, thumb up,
index out, the other three fingers, closed.

We were deprived children! Deprived into adulthood, like all children.

We?

Just words ... words bounced back and forth filling each other's space.

Until?

Until it settles for a moment, say, at dusk, when the tide has reached full and stops for a moment to take stock of itself and the water has stilled to become the mirror of the darkening sky. An old woman has thought of a "snack" for an old man, sitting in an Adirondack chair on the back lawn. The two are intimate strangers. And your guns?

Of the two guns make a frame,
turning one palm toward you
and the other out, and touching
index fingers to thumbs. Your two hands,
once a message to the world, have now
become your frame unto the world.

I am now standing on a low hill
descending into a valley. At the bottom
is the "myriad" as Faulkner might have named it
as he dreamed of the beyond of open wood
and bear, as Whitman or Crane may have
seen it, stepping from a ferry, or crossing
a bridge, or Melville's self-child, spotting
a ship while strapped to a coffin.

Your myriad is bordered on one side
by a mill. Paper, glass, steel? Swirls
of black soot and steam from brick stacks
conflate, blocking our vision.

Or maybe it is the soul of "myriad" rising
smog-like, smudge of an industrial accident.

Farther beyond "myriad" and mill,
the opposite crest of the valley begins
a slow, even ascent to trees, and running
to the side of "myriad" and mill . . . the river
we throw in, just for fun.

I can raise my finger frame now, one hand turned in,
one turned out.

*What will I frame now, what remains in,
what do I leave out: the old forest,
more nameless than ageless — pine,
oak, maple, spruce . . . lichen, fern, moss
— the epochal accumulation of the forest floor:
leaves, insects, bones, all turning to a dark,
moist humus . . . a forest commons of growth,
a turn of the wheel . . . future that is past, a present
devouring the future. And ascending to the mill and myriad:
a white skirt of sapling birch . . . a sycamore quenching
          its thirst?*

*Will I frame the mill there, where it stops forest
dead in its track, straightens the wheel of return,
mixing hope and despair on the playground
of a fearsome future?*

May our fingers frame just a piece of the wood
and a piece of the mill? Not compromise,
rather the battle field. Let the viewer call the shot,
so to speak, what wins, what loses?

Or may the frame focus on the couple
who are now walking away from mill
and "myriad" toward a bank of the river?

*Gratefully, a couple may never know
how they mix their time, with the river's time,
ever expanding, fed by one then another stream
until at its mouth, time is lost in the dance of tides,
neither wheel nor line, but capture and release:
the couple now drifts.*

Drifts. But does the couple have a story?
What do they reveal or fail to reveal
as they drift, unconscious of themselves
as much as of the river, of which
they are not merely a part,

but rather, as in a hologram: the whole
contained in each part, though they are
shattered, whole though they are shattered?
What do we include and leave out
in the field of our joined index fingers and thumbs?
And in the field of each of their minds
whom and what have they included
and left out?

And as for truth?

Have we captured some notion of it
in the frame: what is formed…

or is the essence of truth always
what is left out: what remains unformed?
Formed and formless: Pura poesía:
the smoke and mirror of our daily bread and butter?

And what of our typical denizen of a noonday
street in Madrid?

And what is the name of all that has been left out …
no name without perception

II

Yet my hands, index finger touching thumb, thumb
touching index, seem wanting, or wanting to tell
another story. Inward, each part points to another part,
each a metaphor for another: a race of parts
never to reach the edge of the frame

and metaphorically fall off, fall out?

where, (as we have said) each thing seems "wanting":
a lack of proper names, while the names that remain
to us, as though purloined from a long-defeated language,
seem like rubber globes floating in the air,
maintaining the illusion of shape, though the air
expands and contracts at its pleasure.

Think "Yazo;" think "Nissequogue," or "Hualapai."
Sounds empty of meaning. Adirondacks now
are lawn chairs.

One turned in, one turned out, the one
bearing the vast cargo of the brain: the all
the brain brings as a veil

of cognition?

to what is placed before it
— the other ... this very "what":
the world of seamless affirmation

and negation

of itself ...
the conflation contained within the frame;
electromagnetic field

sparking the universe into life(?)

each part, the sum of all the parts:
hologram (?):

Affirmation/negation delivering itself
to this minuscule puddle between my
indices and thumbs,

like a theory of quanta: what lies in the frame —
the conflation — is there, but where(?) when(?)
a porous frame at best ... calculated
to make us feel good so that even when
all does not end happily it ends "wisely"
— you shake the reins, watch the snow
until your pony signals time to go —

or the mingle of the there and here,
the in the out, like a Mayan painting
on a sacrificial wall: jaguar with a serpent tongue
each point in the split budding into
another jaguar head, the mere becoming:
the mera mera

What do we see now ... thumb to index finger
index to thumb ... world turned in, world tuned out

the mera mera down in old Mexico
removed centuries from the Spanish street
the mera verdad, la mera vida, la mera mierda
— mere truth, mere life, mere shit: the I love you who doesn't look a day
    over thirty-five over fifty over sixty who fights this thing called love
    for I am myself

myself a cancer survivor and who saves the tatas in a tata
       piggy bank for a rainy day and the vaginas and the lonely
       penis hanging like a stem of prostate cancer drowned in
       muddy water blues

and honors father mother god and country guns and guts for you have walked a mile
       in another man's moccasins (though not the mile perhaps that counts)
       or woman's because I never got his name the masked man just rode up
       and truly was back in the saddle again
singing of mermaids who were singing each to each from the shores
       of the endlessly rocking sea mother

four score and seven years ago I John Baptiste see my head floating
       in a convex mirror in a Coney Island house of mirrors
       oh islands of rabbits how far I've become asking not what
       my country will do but what it will do next

asking no questions at all but swallowing each pill the way
       a sword swallower would swallow his swords on the cross
       of lion and lamb I am
       Mary's little lamb fleeced as white as driven snow crossing
          the bridge across these troubled waters laid but never enough and
       laying down the bridge

world bridge across the world London bridge Brooklyn bridge all the
       mera mera pura poesía falling up breathing falling down

III

You are now entering the valley of the shadow
of last appeals — a frame in three dimensions —
where all the world's echoes come to bounce
for a last time, off the last of these red rock walls
and now lie — shards of memory — hushed
in the red sand of the valley floor. Here
only the heat lives turning future into dry
vapor rising up which, as you approach,
becomes silence once more ... dissipates,
disappears. The sky is a blue extension
of the heat. Each rock marks a grave.

Fossils
of ancient sea creatures rise from the rocks,
then, sink back — trilobites, the half-shelled
backbone of an archelon, ancient turtle,
armored fish the size of a contemporary
conundrum the size of a blind alley we
come up against and answer to — long
ago melted into these rocks,
shadows in three dimensions
like the stubborn memory of an old woman,
who, while lying on a gurney in an ER,
is asked the telephone number
of an emergency contact, remembers that
of her son who died twenty maybe thirty
years before. Abruptly, suddenly, as she lies
through the night on the gurney, the numbers
fly before her eyes as if she'd called them
only the night before, while the midnight
nurse tucks her in and asks her how she is:
a shadow made of rock.

<41>

*Pictograms: People have lived here,
have named the silence, painted it in
black on the red walls; the blue silence
of sky, the yellow silence of rocks,
and laughter — a day over, the aroma of
fresh kill roasting in the fire pit;*

*Pick axes, the outline of the foundation
of a hut or cabin; the notion or the smell
or the hope of gold hanging still heavy
over the ruins. West. West. Where the purity
of a dream, the* pura poesía, *washes
away with the dust and the hunger.*

But does it end? Ask the citizens of Madrid,
Barcelona, Sevilla five centuries since
God's Manifest destiny left them where
it all began, in the pigsty of a conquerer's head
left huddled in adobe villages, cold
in Andean torrents, the ice of the altiplano,

took up residence in the holsters
of young cowboys all wrapped in white linen:

leaving a scar across five centuries of time
that cannot cure itself. Ask her, who is now
hanging clothes in the back alley of a tenement
of a city — half dream, half cement —, who
has no time for El Dorado, wetback, gringo
or otherwise, who

sends two small children to school wondering
if they love her, and husband to office wondering
if he loves her or if

today is Thursday and it is raining in Paris
or London or Rome, and sometimes thinks
she'd like to visit, Beijing. Bangkok, or Cusco . . .
"Umbilicus" of beginnings, where, nearby,
a Spaniard, maybe her very ancestor, died
desiccated on a freezing altiplano hill.

But the red walls of this canyon have no answers,
ask no questions.

Then what is it you and I have come so far
to say here?

What can we say here, before meaning moves
on and we are left: mummies with pictographs
in our mouths?

Despite the run of echoes, nuances, words
oozing into other words, does it all come
to rest in a single frame: thumb to index,
index to thumb,

or is it all only this desire, vagrant, bag lady
propped on the steps of The New York Public Library,
main branch, to whose winding mazes she
will retreat tonight and whose restrooms she
will contaminate with her smell
and the smell of her city and of her words

now propped in the shade of one of its lions
and wiping sweat from her forehead as mermaids
pour out from office buildings to eat lunch
in the noon day sun
meet their Ulysses.

                    She is their song
announcing the blue of a small bay
of a small island, its name empty of
meaning, her words filling the space
not to be denied, as language slips
into language, that leaves us behind,
— forgotten or remembered —
living in her desire, framed for this second,
index to thumb, thumb to index.

IV

Now suppose you are in the frame
and someone has handed you a sandwich,
and you are simply an old man
from whom all the old ironies have leaked out,
empty of belief, in a white T-shirt,
blue cotton pants and black shoes
— United States Navy issue, for, after the wars,
these were the only shoes that fit

and suppose your long dead son were,
as usual, beside you, or hanging about
the lilac bush that will soon be in bloom

and suppose you are seated in an Adirondack chair
in your backyard which is situated atop
a slight hummock overlooking a small river
whose fresh waters are now
mixing with the salt waters of a quiet sound
as the tide turns and begins its advance
or retreat, and say

it is an egg salad sandwich on the nutritionless
white bread, before the whole-wheats and multi-grains
and each turn of the tide is a click
you unconsciously record, while,
just as unconsciously you think
or dream or contemplate the last click,
but not now,

for the person who has handed you the sandwich
is the same person who has handed you
many of these same sandwiches and is
the same person whom for many more clicks
you have forgotten if you ever loved her, and if

you have ever loved at all, and if not
loving at all has become a sort
of loving all,

to the degree that you have both been
on this ride before — a short ride
but a happy ride in the end — and
you are sitting side by side
as the ride moves slowly, click by click,
upward to the zenith and the approaching
drop

and suppose further
that this egg salad sandwich on simple white bread
not toasted or altered in any way
since it has left the packages announces
by its simple presence that, by degrees
— click by click — has become your favorite sandwich
with or without the dill pickle
that may or may not have lain beside it
on a simple white platter

and say
if you looked up from the hand handing
you the sandwich to the face and it is a face
you have never seen before — a beautiful face —
and are now seeing for the first time, again,

and say
a stranded word that had lost all its meaning
is now the name of the place where
you were born and the name of the person
who offers you the sandwich,

and it is now reaching out
to some accumulation of meanings,
once lost, and now captured in a mirror
where you find yourself seeing yourself

poor creature that you are — uneasy biped
that you are — twisting yourself into
meaning, meaning this moment,
framing this moment — if only for a moment —
till you don't mean anymore
and simply are? Poet of the purest
poesía?

Hours have passed by now.
It is dark.
The old man remains seated in his Adirondack chair.
He feels the breath of a ghost passing
between an unknown here and an equally
unknown there.
A light shines dimly through the screen door
leading to the kitchen of his bungalow home.
Above him,
the immense plenitude of night,
all around,
the distant whisper of tide waters
flowing in or out.
The screen door squeaks into the silence.
She approaches, white platter in her hands.
"Are you still hungry? Want another sandwich?
This other sandwich?"

WINTERS IN PARIS

WINTERS IN PARIS

(after César Vallejo)

(...) beyond whose enjambered curriculum
vitae stretched the wider shores
of meaninglessness, the hermeneutic
of the empty shell, and the urgent message
interrupting prime time
that takes the lives of all our heroes
and the scrabble children selling oranges between
ticking cars on Guaña Vie from La Paz
to Cusco to Quito and a North-less
town where they are neatly stacked in back alleys
among empty beer cans alleging
they ain't seen nothin'. And, You,
squatting to your morning constitutional
over the common ditch,
midst blaring radio boleros, pathos
of the daily interrogations, and the tremendous B-flats
of the carnal soul, dreaming the islands
left behind and guano, the brown pelicans
like the moments of a passing wave
turned solid, pointed ...
stitching the fabric of the sea
to the fabric of the air;
and you imprisoned in a parched skin
that will not split
here at the edge of a fallow field
and only one unnamed plant
left to grow.

And I said it sounded
"interesting" but needed more ...
and I asked do you mean the way
the long name of things begins sometime
in spring with a first syllable sung
from the depths of a quiet ocean? Once,
I continued,
we were all climbing caracol stairs,
some in our marvelous feather hats, some
on our hands and knees, whilst all about
the trains and buses were lined
up waiting. It was the last green tour leaving
the city: the crumbling picnic tables,
the topped off mountains, packed lunch
baskets, bread and butter. From the side lines
we cheered the passing faces, the drummer,
bugler boys, majorettes, our faces, the creeping
floats, heavy in dreams, coming home (who
had we knowingly, unknowingly been
raped? coming home?)
    ... whose word was left
to linger at the edge of the one way
floating bridge. Some time into
the confusion, the children had gotten lost
or struggled to say something. The interrogations
proceeded on schedule under the suspects'
nails. Their hearts would be cleansed
in the sun at daybreak and distributed
accordingly — the goddess snake,
unshed, lay dead in the gutter,
her tongue, limp fork,
seeping from her lips.

KNOTS

How long have I lived
this *other* song   Today:
discordant knot but will you
love me tomorrow   Strangers
from a diminished South
waited for the season's new mates
from the branches of renewed trees
— their songs, waking my heart —
and I thought of the song
"Peg o' My Heart." Only the real song
began there in no words, lying for years
undead, "un-alive"
hoping to be only to be
(the way a serpent slips her skin
and shiny is someone else)   filling
the four drums of my heart
with its heady though perhaps unhealthy
self asking to be sung anyway — and
"I feel I must sing and dance"   in
a plural me, the plural of you — like
a stray need scratching at the door
asking only for warm clothes and to be
fed a hot meal   making it clear in return
there'd be no return. Then, back then,
I was a galley of words   old
man in diapers for pants when
you appeared soft, calming my leeward
and I fed you stories milked in bread

I never expected more   then, by then, we'd
already bred ourselves into ourselves
each a separate game of chance
waiting to hatch   Dream
of continuance we wove from
memories embedded in sand
the restless stamp of waves.
We spent a summer of lifetime, thumbing
through pages of shoreline for words
for our song, no matter what was
or was not to keep for ourselves
as we slipped from ourselves
even the night across
the mist planks of an unmoored bridge
a sea of wishes below
a hush of ascending cables
and we like two fine notes
plucked and trembling at the edges.

LONG NAME

El nombre exacto de la cosa
—(Juan Ramón Jiménez)

Like reading to where you don't know it
anymore   I break into an FB post
on the care and breeding of small creatures
small, fuzzy and suddenly, utterly senseless
next to *"cara mia* hear my plea"
as you sift me back to an essence
of my self that can't wait   a loan
unpaid in the erotic sense
a recent ghost has of reclaiming
your favorite armchair for herself   reading words
denied syntax   like islands left
behind in someone else's poem
(who's making all that racket?)   you/me
a balloon on eggshell strings   then
"I was thinking of whales or wheels
solid bits of enunciation   weightless
in prisms of ocean   their organs
and body functions a question responding
to depth and pressure"   and they sing
their long name   thread of light through dark
and silence in a way I wish to sing you
tempered in ocean and longing
one may find one's own particular name
on a beach or piece of lint left
on a rag of clothing to be worn
in a hastily plumbed future   name

we forget as we speak   have
forgotten over the long time exact name
of the thing   leaked
through a crack in the words
like a stain through a white concrete
wall   welcome ghost

Hear your bread dipped in holy oil
I've made you your coffee

REJOICE, LAMB

Who hasn't maimed — or been
maimed — at least once by a close
relative or trusted member
of the community — is to a poem
as three capsules of life hung from
a tree limb in the dearth of winter
— I'll take two capsules, please,
but please don't call me in the morning — is
to an aspirin taken for reasons of the heart   as
who, having lived once and lost — is
to a vow hung out to dry
like a white sheet in the morning sun.
So, who is peeking over my shoulder now?
For the train is crowded enough
You are not allowed
For this poesy is a larger ferry yet
subject to — sinkable at — the slightest
whim of literary review, or huff
of biblical exegesis
For is this poem as pure as the stare
in in the eyes of praying cat
For it is wider and deeper than what it knows
and knows no afterglow
of the last lonely survivor   For you,
sweet remnant of youth, have fought
a fine and noble war, suffocated
in record heat at the sound of taps
counting the remaining digits
on your frozen hands and feet

FALLING

(in memoriam)

Late that night from inside we heard the buzzing,
accumulation of all the dead-talk;
it was a mosquito, the one wing of
a cricket rasping. The inexcusable,
at least,
the unforgivable had occurred and
you needed more than just one transfusion
to raise your voice above the silence. Why
do moms behave like that, we asked ourselves,
and why lie hidden in the plural when
it was the single I among so many shadows?
So it was the "I" … nothing really, some-
thing to say as much to please the unknown
friends we message as to please one's self
— as when you close your eyes in front of a mirror
to remember self. And so it behooved us
(behooved us?) not to rend our clothes in view
of the ocean ahead. The most erudite words
had to be lifted from the color box
and honed to precision — longer the better —
to support the makeshift cantilever.
For a time we were allowed time to see
syllables of joy filling the night sky
and distant horizon. They were her passing.
Signs could be sent as long as fingers could
scratch and mouths utter. Here was the blood.
Caress me, mother, tell me your truth.

NEW YORK
IN AUTUMN

NEW YORK IN AUTUMN

(In memoriam)

You like Spring best who are not you
anymore. It went through your growing hair
like a notion too quickly gone for an idea
to catch up, but wakes you in the middle
of a season not Spring — the sudden burst
of a Christmas cactus, the sun's not
scheduled descent
through a hospital window. Yet for some reason,
you were always going, expert
at finding the next dream party, the next
friend to befriend, the white cat
with the one tan stain on his head; expert
at climbing into the back seat of a taxi — "Where to,
my friend?" The city is so big ... anywhere,
anywhere. Today grackles,
redwing blackbirds, starlings fill
the trees like dark ghosts of leaves yet to bud.
You have donned the fedora you never take off
anymore, have a cigarette between your fingers
as your eyes always light, always wise
follow the yellow taxis Eastward, Westward,
all around the town.

AQUARELLE

(In memoriam)

Mountains were not his "thing."
"Home" was more the slice of prows through white splash
and spume, the canvas spearhead of a sail
through sun-washed sky. Later came a profusion
of flowers, the tropical pinks of lilies,
or a Key West home and garden. But not
the progress of stone. So that when he works on
the meander of green and brown foothills,
the austere rise of blue and white snowcapped peaks
to clouds and sky — each demanding its own
integrity of place, time — mass becomes
the climate of his now empty home. How,
then, to produce in the wash of aquarelles
the gravity of stone? Business stops. All
else comes to rest. History is invested
in how shear bulk may touch sky, how sky
dissolves rock to mist and blue space.
The artist of color (or words) is confronted with
a concept, an idea, say, or "feel." Stone
becomes the subject of liquidity,
the tentative touch of a brush: an affair
before it knows it is love. The painter is
at home now in the weight of mountains. Mountains
find their home in clouds.

GLOSS ON A GLOSS

" ... the truth inside meaning"
— (from the jacket cover of *Shadow Train*, by John Ashbery)

What they printed on the jacket must be
true. Dressed in the indicative, we may close
that door — where you were, who you are, and
the fine lecture on poetry you delivered in
the hall of ancient humanities and mirrors.
We all came to this place as if led by
a seventh sense to the bottom of pain
and pleasure where clothes don't feel
right anymore. Much wider landscapes live
on this other side of syntax, though even then
only as ghosts frozen in a reflection pool.
You know what I mean — you must go
back to the magic drawer in Grandma's
crowded china closet. What she's forgotten
there you must rummage through one Sunday
over and over, for lives depend on it,
perhaps not yours who are grown up now,
then whose? In the adjacent world
the lecture seemed never to end and then
there were sandwiches, crustless, cut
into tiny sailboats. We could sail
away though never be sure of what lay
in those pelagic coves, for what becomes
of it lives in another mood — the side
most distant from the shore's lighthouse. If
it is the same drift of worlds that brought
us here bathing in the sand like half drowned
swimmers, let it please you that
that same truth trickle from behind
into being, like the remains

of a counter spill the sponge
could not absorb and squeeze down
into the drain.

Please you that we live this way
"mirthful" waiving what looms
behind us like a persistent head cold,
ink blot on a page
or a shadow.

YOU SAW THE END

(In memoriam)

You saw the end coming.
I saw a trolley taking us
to a botanical garden that never ends, open
to the public; rust and yellow mums
blooming as the season reaches its edge
— and one, the reddest afterthought, placed there
as on a sword.
Yet we both knew somewhere of the motion picture
in which we are seated watching a motion picture
in which we are seated. How
your image migrates now. Your hair
and eyes — as if all that were left
were hair and eyes sowed into the illicit
reliquaries old women patched together
from pieces of red silk. Tiny silk pillows
stuffed with cotton and bone on which
to lay a dream. True, it was all
plastic dinosaurs on Saturdays
and trips downtown. Any child
and her sister could squat at the edge
of the world to play pick-up jacks.
Nothing to hold as each thing was
self and only self. Night went by
like liquid air though a water thief.
Are you asleep now? Is there another
flower continent to be wondered about
or wandered through?

SATURDAYS

(In memoriam)

If someone raps at the door, remember,
this home is not our home — like children
of grim tides we succumb to the furniture
not wanting to be kneaded into bread
or forgotten either. I am mostly
a wandering salesman selling haberdashery on
Saturdays to poor and needy Long Island housewives,
door to door who have come to these shores,
starvation burning holes in our pockets.
— Sundays, I drink coffee from paper cups;
friendly Jewish store-keeps on Delancey Street
treat me to knishes as I buy nice white shirts
for school kids, and red, nylon underwear
for their mothers.
My name is Sal;
they laugh and call me Sol.
At times, crossing the bridge
between wholesale stores and home,
I see stocks of pigeons
flights and tipplers mostly
crossing also.
Streets shine like a market place
and all things hanging in the air are someone's
object of obscure desire — the old women among us,
unrequited lives woven like bandages
or badges into their laps. We succeed among
the failure in nourishing our bodies though
a history before time warns this place
was not meant for us

as though a crime committed long ago
had wrapped us in its arms and brought
us back to rehash the county coroner's
preliminary findings.
No matter, we may go out now
buying and selling our wares.
They won't see us anyway.
We are all ghosts anyway.

ROCCA DI NETO— STONE ON THE RIVER

YOU OLD DOG YOU

The passage rising from nowhere
and descending to nowhere keeps
the empty bottle full of white sails
and painted shards.
Ahead, the *castra* bracing themselves
against the next breed of Normans
(make that Saracens) create their own fantasy:
receding shores, days receding
like an old man's hair line.
You, my friend, are nothing to look at
anymore, or smell either in the heat
of your fading moments, yet the aroma
of a strange cake rising from the distant
central island keeps your wet nose poised
against the window, wags your tail
opening this parenthetical lull in the blue
landscape of gently eroding waves
— your mind, the frame in which
the picture is told, asleep,
evolves into your personal
mirage of distance contained in beauty.
I'm telling you this
as if from the next rise
or fall in the breeze, like
the hand writing you now
I pine for you, crave for my own
the special embrace of your many loves.

At the great illusory juncture of things,
hearts, minds and loins weigh
commingle in the tinted glow
of the Grandscape of things
— we are moony tonight like a beggar
sitting in poverty upon great wealth.
    I kiss both your cheeks
    and beseech you.

SISTINE CHAPEL

Not that all the signs weren't there
promising to the faithful eyes to see
platters laden with Tiberis fat
but wise binoculars reveal the ecstasy
between those fingers who never touch
— did Basho dream that, the dream
of the frog's plump surface breaching
the surface of the pond, or after the rush
of tours through rooms on painted room,
may we only think of a hearty
pasta and maiale lunch?

   … as if the project of a city — any city —
isn't launched on a raft of lilies mourning
in advance (Did you really think to find
or lose yourself somehow on a postcard
or a plow-blade buried in a stony river bed?)
   … yet you've dreamed of this already,
even before the roads winding
though these hills, the footsteps of Roman
farmers through these Tiber River beds.

Look now:
the silence filled with young girls thumbing
messages into smart phones, taking photos
of holy stasis, set in frescos on the walls …
somehow it has always been
about their fleeting eyes and veils.
Yet the myth we must invent to grasp
the myths displayed before us is
always personal, created for the moment,

the way the meaning of home
is always home is personal
or a river. Besides
what do I know about the union of plaster and color,
the yearning of a surface for a surface, privy only,
as I am, to painted shards of poems
and cell phone conversation.

CASTEL DELL'OVO — BAY OF NAPLES

Somewhere in the 15th Century something
Spanish happened here. There were precedents:
Virgil disguised as a wizard placed an egg
in the base to make it eternal. Greeks
went about naming the new metropolis
and the rhythm like the tides was set.
Wasn't that Pulcinella with the black mask,
white clothes and mirrors for eyes? Truly,
I knew this water from times before I was born,
turned over each stone in the bay searching
for dinner or a Saracen dagger. We
descended with our sheep, planted madonnas
in grottoes where the ancient virgins once
had called ... makes it all be more
want more like a date
on a calendar that never comes because
it never changes, but sends out webs
of music: drone of zampognas, sting
of the spider — we dance. And yes,
these streets may be dangerous — little gods
make it this way and no great god to change it,
like a heart beating within a volcano. Time
after time, old men will sit down on rocks
trying to screw back all the missing pieces.
Some far away, we write
in different tongues, still as ornaments
under Christmas tree. You've seen them:
old women selling chestnuts, young boy
chasing a goat (I am the shoemaker's son).

Take one. If you hold it by the right edge,
spinning stops for a moment, and for a moment
you come to who you are. You were born
under a fig tree neither here nor there.
For years you were a little fig
and now you are a big fig,
hard and gold and sweet on a stick.

ROCCA DI NETO: STONE ON THE RIVER

It didn't mean to be so,
or, for that matter, otherwise ...
like the river itself bending at the skirt
of the hill-town, finding its own level
and time. It wants you to know something
about these dirt floors, recently covered
with marble, the imported cherry furniture,
the stone laid streets that flow into
dirt paths at the olive groves. Like
the Ionic Sea, shining in the distance,
barely kilometers from sunrise, daring you not
to see the green clarity of it all, and
the rock crab half crawling, half gliding
to the shadow of those rocks. But as always
the next war came, another hero, child-
novice — your blood relative and ours —
sent here not wholly of his will, riding a mule
to the coast town to trade his "funny" stories
for food and clothes for the old ones
in the language of the enemy, who
were now our friends and saved the town
— you say he died of loneliness and priesthood;
yet voices whispered in circles of old women
honor and endure him just the same. Was easier
always to laugh even with no teeth
and dream of better times.
It sinks on to you: midday in the sunlight
of the empty piazza, like a handful of dirt
so far, so far the eye blurs and
it is you today and tomorrow.

You see the picture now, the pattern: war-lost Trojans,
memory strapped to their backs, Greeks and their unyielding,
unforgiving virgin goddess, blond Normans,
white robed Saracens ...
the young Sri Lankan stepping from the
train with his wares ... talk to them,
they know you.

Spider dance — "tarantella" —
our ghosts dance each night
on the holy ground (they can't do otherwise)
the spiral cakes we eat for Christmas Solstice
In honor of the Christ and She-Snake
— Roman Goddess ... They are eternal.
Talk to them. We listen ... and this kiss
for both your cheeks. We can't do otherwise.

LE CASTELLA — CROTONE PROVINCE

These are sketches — nothing more — like the day
your steel helmet lands on a beachhead and
from your half-sand, half-panicked trench, you fix
on a white seagull perched on a land mine.
The year is Aragonese or German;
you may not say who you are, or cannot.
The main thread eludes us or was
never written, or lives in the woven confines
of a recipe book: she-spider
and her *pasqual* eggs. Where to advance
from here? Windmills on the hill saturate
the horizon; families settle down to the *pranzo*, "good
things are on the way." Your shadow remains
as you push on. At beachheads they built strings
of *castra* to protect the towns against
invading armies. Now only the wind
prevails and her many jealous lovers
the waves. Green grocers only sell the fruit
of the season — honest folk — but when I looked,
it was me looking through the mirror. We
then marched through fields of new fennel, the
top of each plant, like a soft green fur mourning
the blood enriching the ground. No romance
here or the pleasure of true religion,
only the ghosts of old women dancing
the dust from the burial place. And we
dance to this rhythm now, flailing our arms
and legs like spiders climbing the wind. Peace
follows as it always does — judgment as
ceaseless as it is meaningless. The gull,
born to better things, lifts away. The steel
in your brain embraces the fragile calm.

RISO AMARO

A suspect presence of form
without matter, an empty storage hold
in the galley of the mind for a knowing
before knowing, shaped in the form
of knowing … may one day be traced
to a random snip of DNA, slipped
— decidedly unwanted — into your double helix:
affiliation with old soils, memories of passion
played out in brown hills through dry times: nostalgia
lives here, though you have not. Suspension
of belief is the norm, comic … desultory;
choice is yours. These sidewalk kiosks
are full of green beans, for instance,
escarole and figs, all fresh,
ripened on the vine, all in season — like us —,
some not … as if
the severed head of your favorite language poet
had stolen into the cantaloupe exhibit,
disguised as a notepad, had slipped into
your grammar and purloined your tongue … is
now cruising down the Champs-Élysées, or
squatting in a dungeon along the fog-
lost coast of the southeastern Pacific …
has changed to white p-j's and a black mask
to sniff a po'-boy on Fat Tuesday
on St. Francis Street.

Traveling north from stone towns,
Apulean hills pass by
as if worn down from age alone
beyond ticked-time and erosion. No outbreaks
of malaria, real or forgotten, no armies today
or the face of another unfamiliar god
— the narrow vias of Foggia are made
only for lovers wishing nothing more
than to copulate, to taste the rich and
intensely familiar cheeses, with red
wines in the afternoon
                      and for writers
as if, up and down the coast and valleys
the memory of old lords and bitter rice
were all legend, fun and bitter laughter.

Now, there are distant hills, groves of olive,
day pilgrimages and picnics of the poor
in the Shadow of the Black Madonna
— *L'Incoronata* —, reconciliation
of the people to her soil.
And I listen from the outcrop
of my topography to next rooms brimming
with ancient foods and conversation, not
knowing melons from the portraits they speak.
They say that until today it almost
never rains, though memory is often
kept on a short leash.
They say that tourists come and tourists go
to the heartbeat of the spider dance,
agendas of travel and longing tucked
in their pockets.

ARRIVING AT POMPEII

*To Kay Fineran Luthin, who organizes our weekly get-togethers
in this very small town tucked into Penn's Woods*

Islands of words list behind us
— the place at the edge of language
lingers in storage that we may first sit
to fatted calf parts — returning prodigals —
and tacos with best friends, drinking in
wine-tossed seas at the local Mexican
restaurant, behind the lobby of this
extended stay hotel. Except

for the losses — people, things —the drawn-out
wait breathing from discreet, brown paper
wrappings of memory, life continues
— even-keeled: moments when I thought
of nothing more than regional salamis,
aromatic cheeses, inlets, bays with scenic views,
the sea beyond. From the street bordering

the Gulf of Naples, we tourists took selfies
with Vesuvius — Leopardi's "Sterminator" —
in the background, never close enough to see
the yellow broom flowers softening old lava
like asphodels sprung from the acrid soil
of the Jersey Pine Barrens: two flowers,
two worlds.

Over sweet and salty margaritas
— little daisies — you ask me and I tell
you, Pompeii is a time to be toyed with: grid
of streets and squares, once homes ... wine and
cheese shops, shops of all the world's exotica
and houses of paid and passing pleasures:

the Roman aesthetic fettered in logic and
symmetry, pressed into an uneasy ground.
The grid remains, the structures are mainly rubble
half filling half empty squares ... reminds me

— mere observer —
of nothing than a game of patsy played
on empty numbered boxes chalked
on the sidewalk of a larger and more
complicated city, where "Cutie" at eight
and Cecilia at ten played, dropped
hairpins into one square, then jumped through
the map, as I watched ... intimations
of sex before knowledge, the structure
of lust before the labyrinth of guilt:

game with no endgame, designed for leisurely
walks among flowers and fountains ... patricians
on holiday, Greeks and African sailors
on leave from the sea: a memory of
casual pleasure to take home and lock
safely in a seaman's trunk.

The tourists had all lined up, speaking awe
in the sincerest sentences of their respective
languages. I took my turn speaking words
learned before speech.

We followed the patient docent to
the Venus Gate. Pompeii was her city
— virgin of the eternal, renewed each season
like a broom or asphodel, who softens
the wrath of the gods and god. Below us

the wine purple gulf was much closer
though all was much the same: vendors,
both picturesque and picaresque, booklets
on shrines to visit, maps of cities to see,
meals on the run, yet strangely nutritious,
taken with a sense of pleasure
that could not leave them.

Somehow the millennia had changed,
yet all had remained the same.

Somehow the port was in sight.
The uncomplicated port was in sight.

ABOUT THE POEMS

    I have lived most of my life between two continents: North and South America. As one would suspect, therefore, there is a degree of "Spanglish" not only in the language of these poems but in the allusions to South American poets: namely, Cesar Vallejo and Pablo Neruda, but mostly Vallejo, much of whose poetry borders the line of what is possible to express in words and the inexpressible that waits just beyond. John Ashbery, at least to me, is another voice that trails off in the same direction, though, perhaps without the emotional charge of Vallejo, once imprisoned in Peru, and later to experience hunger and poverty in Paris.

    Juan Ramón Jiménez, a Spanish poet, asked in his poetry for the name of things (*el nombre exacto de las cosas*). And this exact name, the one we may never pronounce, is what I allude to in these poems: the long name of things, the name that is born with us at our birth and grows as we grow and dies with us when we die. This is the name that defines us or identifies us at our essence — if there is an essence.

    There is another continent involved in these poems; at least a continent of the mind: Italy, which I visited while writing this book. As a thoroughly "hyphenated" American, the country of my grandparents, their town (Rocca di Neto), as they are, is always there and is not there: a presence felt mostly as an absence. A country (maybe only a town) grew to be a continent because it has been with me since my birth in the foods they prepared, the stories they told or refrained from telling. I grew up with ways of thinking that were not "wholly" American but rather had leaked into my consciousness — perhaps my conscience — through other sources. The last part of the book deals with other sources and their meanings. For instance, the "tarantella" is not the "folksy" stereotypical dance with which an Italian American wedding ends. Its rhythm is hypnotic. Its purpose is to put the dancers into a trance in which rituals of life and death are reenacted: moments of love, of passion, of honor. Its name refers to a tarantula — really a large spider — because within the trance the dancers thrash around their arms and legs like those of a frenzied spider. Thus, my aim was to "de-stereotype" the dance and "reveal" its original "mystery."

Heidegger writes that for the Greeks, truth was revelation. Thus I wished in these poems to unveil certain truths about my people and about myself.

Of course, to reveal a "mystery" is really to discover another veil. And sometimes only irony can balance this paradox. In the last poem, the ground plan of Pompeii, for all its symmetry and planning, reminded me of the game of patsy the young girls in my childhood neighborhood once played. Thus it brought me home:

> Somehow the port was in sight.
> The uncomplicated port was in sight.

I am indebted to the poet and critic Roberto Bonazzi for his commentaries and suggestions regarding the order in which these poems appear.

ABOUT THE POET

Vincent Spina was born in Brooklyn, New York. He received his Ph.D. from New York University in Latin American and Brazilian Literature, and is a Professor Emeritus of Modern Languages and Cultures. His poems have appeared in various magazines over the years, and his first book of poetry, *Outer Borough*, was published in 2008. He is also the author of *El Modo Epico en José María Arguedas*, a study of the Peruvian author's novels and their basis in the cosmology of the Andean people of Peru. His articles on Latin American writers have also appeared in magazines and anthologies.

ABOUT THIS BOOK

The text of this book is set in Centaur, a classic, Renaissance-inspired typeface from the hot metal era. It was first designed in capital letters only by Bruce Rogers in 1914. The completed type family with lower-case letters and italics was released by Monotype in 1929. It has been a popular face with fine presses, and is still used for many letterpress productions. The title-page and section headings are in Futura, a Bauhaus-influenced type that came to be one of the most popular sans-serif faces used in the 20th century. Its geometric emphasis and even width of stroke takes its form from classic Greek column lettering, but looks completely modern because of its strict use of geometric forms (circles and isosceles triangles). The hot metal face was designed in 1927 for the Bauer foundry in Germany. The cover art, which is also the basis of section ornaments, is a 2014 Conte crayon drawing by Pieter Vanderbeck, "Sunrise at Lost Pond."

www.ingramcontent.com/pod-product-compliance
Lightning Source LLC
Chambersburg PA
CBHW051700040426
42446CB00009B/1233

LYRA
THE PRINCESS OF PROVIDENCE

Lyra Brown Nickerson
Her Life and Legacy

By

Clive Nickerson

© Copyright 2024 by Clive Nickerson - All rights reserved.
It is not legal to reproduce, duplicate, or transmit any part of this document in either electronic means or printed format. Recording of this publication is strictly prohibited.

Copyright @2024 by Clive Nickerson

All rights reserved. No part of this book may be reproduced in any form or by electronic or mechanical means, including information storage or retrieval systems, without permission from the publisher.

ISBN 979-8-218-80664-4

Nickerson, Clive L., 1941-
LYRA:THE PRINCESS OF PROVIDENCE/Clive Nickerson

Printed and bound by Lulu.com in the United States of America
First printing 2025

Self published by Clive Nickerson

This book is dedicated to:

Dacia (Libutti) Nickerson
Dacia and Hera Votolato
Matthew and Thomas Nickerson

Cover Photograph and Signature from U.S. Passport Applications, Roll 229, 1915 Dec-Jan, Cert. 46116, Image 360, found through Familysearch.com

Contents

Contents v
List of Figures vii
Introduction ix
PART I: Lyra's Early Years 1
  1. The Family 1
    The Patriarch 1
    The Parents 2
    The Providence Art Club 3
    Alice Lahey 6
    The Debutante 7
    Gilded Age Girls 7
  2. The Heiress 10
    The Will of Joseph Rogers Brown 10
    The Wills of Lyra F. Nickerson and Edward I. Nickerson 10
    The Art Treasures of Edward I. Nickerson 11
    The Will of Jane Frances Brown 13
    Saving Angell Street 15
    Richard B Comstock 18
PART II: Lyra The Woman 19
  1. The Socialite 19
    The Princess of Providence 19
    Narragansett Pier 23
    'Immigrant' Ball 25
    Kitty Schermerhorn 26
    Weddings 26
    The Tennis Court 27
    Black and White Balls 31

The Lacey-Bakers	34
2. The Philanthropist	**37**
The Nickerson Settlement House	37
Belgian Relief	41
The Irrepressible Society	41
3. The Spy	**43**
The European Adventure	43
Who was Conway Evans?	49
4. The Aviatrix	**51**
5. The Betrothed	**57**
6. The Tragedy	**62**
7. The Legacy	**67**
Special Bequests	67
Henry Garfield Clark	68
Alice Lahey Foster	69
Providence Public Library and RISD	70

Epilogue/Conclusion	*73*
She Was a Phantom of Delight	*74*
Appendix A: Family Ties	*75*
Appendix B: Nickerson Designed Houses	*77*
Bibliography	*79*
Acknowledgments	*81*
About the Author	*0*

List of Figures

1. Lyra Brown Nickerson ix
2. Joseph Rogers Brown 1
3. Lyra Frances Brown 2
4. Edward I. Nickerson 2
5. Carr House 3
6. Edward Silhouette 4
7. 71 Angell Street 5
8. Helen Ostby 8
9. Egyptian Canopic Jar   10. Italian Slippers .. 11
11. Piranesi Etching 12
12. The Jane Brown Hospital 13
13. Browns Headstone 14
14. John R. Freeman 15
15. Theodore Francis Green 17
16. Margeret Hawkesworth and Partner 22
17. Kentara Green 23
18. Kentara Cottage 24
19. Lucia Chase and Antoinette Bloodgood 25
20. Bill Tilden 28
21. Smoking Molla 29
22. Black and White Lyra 32
23. Marjorie Lacey-Baker (center) 35
24. The Imperator 36
25. Grace Memorial Home 37
26. The Nickerson House 38
27. Nickerson House Playroom 38
28. Cooking Class 39
29. Lyra   30. Kitty   31. Conway Evans 43
32. The Escape Route 47
33. Challenged by Flagship 48
34. SS Kroonland in the Panama Canal -February 1915 .. 50
35. Hupmobile   36. Scripps-Booth 51
37. Sturtevant Seaplane 52
38. Lyra Ready for Takeoff 53
39. Lyra and R.W. Wright Over Narragansett Bay 53
40. Raymond Estey and "Lyra" 54

41. Aviatrix	55
42. At Quonset	56
43. Henry Clark	60
44. Notice of Passing	63
45. Memorial Plaque	64
46. With the "Boys"	65
47. Swan Point Gravestone	66
48. Henry and Marjorie	68
49. Lyra Nickerson Foster	69
50. Jewelry Bench Room	71
51. Perfect Woman	73
52. Arnold House	77

Introduction

Lyra Brown Nickerson's life bridged the 19th century Gilded Age to the early 20th century Progressive Era. Lyra left a legacy that will never be matched in the State of Rhode Island. She used her $6,000,000 fortune to leave a huge endowment to build the Providence Public Library System and to be largely responsible for the creation of the Rhode Island School of Design Museum. Her personal life was no less noteworthy. She was a pioneer in aviation and famous promoter of tennis in Rhode Island. Lyra's overseas adventures included being arrested as a spy at the outbreak of World War I. Her social events were reported in society pages of newspapers across the nation.

1. Lyra Brown Nickerson[1]

---

[1] Cutter, William Roland ed. *American Biography, A New Cyclopedia, Vol. 6.*

Lyra was born in 1885 to parents who lived in the affluent College Hill neighborhood on the east side of Providence. Her father Edward was a major Providence architect and her mother, another Lyra, was the heiress to the Joseph Rogers Brown fortune. Their wealth did not reach the heights of their Newport contemporaries such as Cornelius Vanderbilt of the Breakers Mansion, but they were certainly among the upper crust of Providence Gilded Age society. Those times were noted for the huge material gap between the haves and have nots. The Nickersons did live an advantaged life, travelling internationally frequently where Edward amassed a large collection of valuable antique artifacts during their sojourns. Young Lyra accompanied her parents on many occasions.

When Lyra reached maturity, the Progressive Era was in full swing. President Theodore Roosevelt epitomized the times and espoused the "strenuous life" for the leisure class. Teddy felt that the more affluent should not take the easy path. Like many of her generation, Lyra felt she owed much because of her means-*noblesse oblige*. She became an avid philanthropist giving freely to several incipient causes in Rhode Island and eventually left a legacy of most of her wealth to outside institutions rather than her relatives and friends. Lyra made an indelible mark on Providence and Rhode Island. Her spirited approach led many to admire her as a popular and "strenuous" heiress.

There was a special place in the Olneyville village in Providence called the Nickerson House that benefitted local children. Dacia Libutti who later became a Nickerson, the author's wife, was one of many children that reaped the benefits. Dacia first learned to play the piano there and went on to perform on Providence WJAR radio. She recalls a picture on the wall of the Nickerson House of a very pleasant looking woman. That woman was the Center's benefactor-Lyra Brown Nickerson. Dacia looked up at the image of this remarkable person with extreme admiration and gratitude. Little did she know at the time of Lyra's extraordinary life - a woman way before her time.

~ x ~

PART I: Lyra's Early Years

1. The Family

The Patriarch

2. Joseph Rogers Brown[2]

    Lyra's grandfather, Joseph Rogers Brown, was the founder of Brown and Sharpe and was the source of the fortune that she eventually inherited. He married twice, first to Caroline Nils, Lyra's maternal grandmother, and later to Jane F. Mowry.

    Joseph Rogers Brown, inventor and entrepreneur, was an important contributor to the "Second Industrial Revolution" in the latter half of the 19th century. He transformed his father's clockmaking and job shop business into a giant in the field of manufacturing equipment and industrial measurement tools. Joseph perfected the precision vernier caliper and invented a universal milling machine. Partnering with Lucien Sharpe, his company's products certainly helped establish mass production and the introduction of interchangeable parts vital to the emerging auto industry among others. Joseph died in 1876 leaving great wealth from the success of Brown and Sharpe.

---

[2] Cutter, William Roland ed. *New England Families, geological and memorial, Vol.3*.

The Parents

3. Lyra Frances Brown   *4. Edward I. Nickerson*

Lyra Brown Nickerson was an only child, born on December 7th 1885 into one of the most prestigious families in Providence. All four of her natural grandparents were deceased at the time of her birth. Her mother, Lyra Frances Brown, was heir to the fortunes of the founders of Brown and Sharpe, a company that manufactured precision measurement devices for industry. Edward Irving Nickerson, Lyra's father, was a renowned Rhode Island architect who designed many of the iconic Queen Anne style homes (See Appendix B: Nickerson Designed Houses) in Rhode Island and was a direct descendant of the original settler of Chatham, Massachusetts - William Nickerson.[3] Lyra's parents were members of the Grace Episcopal Church in Providence where Lyra was confirmed as a member in 1903.[4] Grace Church was considered at that time the most fashionable and wealthiest congregation in Providence. Edward's father, Sparrow Howes Nickerson, was born in South Dennis, Massachusetts on Cape Cod on the 5th of April, 1821. Sparrow's father, Mulford Nickerson, moved the family to Pawtucket, Rhode Island, circa 1821. Sparrow married Elizabeth Clarke Darling of Mendon South Parish (now Blackstone), Massachusetts in 1844. After the death of Elizabeth in 1879, Sparrow remarried in 1880. His second wife, Julia Congdon Bourn, lived for decades after Sparrow's 1881 death. Sparrow, Elizabeth and Julia are resting in peace together in Providence's Swan Point Cemetery.

---

[3] Anthony, O. Dale, personal correspondence.
[4] Rhode Island School of Design Museum, images.

The Dr. George W. Carr House on the corner of Benefit and Waterman Streets in Providence is an example of Edward I. Nickerson's distinctive designs. It now is part of the Rhode Island School of Design and a Providence landmark. Edward also designed the Grace Memorial Home on Delaine Street in Olneyville, original home of the Providence Day Nursery Association - the forerunner of the Nickerson House (see Part II, Chapter 2, The Philanthropist).

5. *Carr House*

The Providence Art Club

Angell Street (named for Thomas Angell, a property owner in the area and an associate of Roger Williams) terminates at Benefit Street as one descends College Hill. Proceeding across Benefit, a small extension originally called Angell's Lane and now named Thomas Street continues down the Hill to North Main Street. The Providence Art Club is housed in four adjacent buildings on Thomas Street opposite one side of the First Baptist Church.

The Providence Art Club was formed in 1880 by a group of artists and art connoisseurs to foster art appreciation in the city. Six years later, the Club signed a lease for 11 Thomas Street and moved into the building at that address, a brick front originally built by Seril Dodge and once occupied by Obadiah Brown who had received the home as a gift

---

[5] https://digitalcommons.risd.edu/,*Bulletin of the Rhode Island School of Design*, Vol. IV, N. 3, July 1916.

from his father Moses Brown. The building came to be known as the Seril House II, the Brick House and the Club House.

Before the Art Club moved in January 1887, Lyra's father and Art Club Treasurer Edward I. Nickerson was called upon to redesign the interior of the Club House. Among his alterations was the combining of the second and third floors and addition of a skylight to create a spacious upstairs art gallery. Obadiah's dining room was turned into the "Green Room" by sheathing the walls with house shutters and adding a chimney and fireplace. Again in 1896, Edward's plans were used for Club House revisions. Edward designed an addition to the rear of the building to accommodate the needs of the members including a "Grill Room" aka dining room.

A tradition in the Club House was started in the early years of the Art Club to have informal Friday meetings around the fireplace where a group of members held discussions and talks in the spirit of camaraderie. The confab group was dubbed the "Friday Knights" and in 1887, forty-four of these patriarchs including Nickerson had their names burnt into the Green Room table by a hot poker. In addition, their silhouettes were drawn on the plaster walls using candlelit shadows.[6]

Edward I. Nickerson

6. Edward Silhouette

After the deed of the Club House was ceded to the Providence Art Club in 1906, a Dutch Kitchen was built to meet the needs of the "Friday Knights." Edward's daughter Lyra donated a set of Persian tiles which were set in plaster panels under a plate rail supported by curved half timbers.

---

[6] Minor, George Leland, *Angell's Lane, the History of a Little Street in Providence.*

Edward I. Nickerson was also a trustee of the Providence Public Library, and in 1890 was the President of the Rhode Island Horticultural Society. Under his leadership, the Society held an impressive exhibition of roses and strawberries at Infantry Hall on South Main Street with music by the 22-piece D. W. Reeves American Band.[7]

Lyra Brown Nickerson grew up as a privileged child in their Angell Street home in Providence. The family had two Irish servants and travelled internationally on a regular basis. She had private tutors at an early age and later attended the private Lincoln School on Thayer Street operated by Misses Ednah Bowen and Margaret Gilman. Lyra was born and bred on Angell Street in Providence and 71 Angell Street[8] became her home for her entire life. The spacious three-story building is on the corner of Prospect Street and is only about 500 feet from Brown University's Van Wickle Gates. It is now known as Larned House and is a residence hall for the Rhode Island School of Design.

7. 71 Angell Street

---

[7] Providence Journal, *Music and Roses*, June 20, 1890, p.3.
[8] Wikipedia Commons image.

Alice Lahey

Alice Lahey of Mongomery, Alabama was described in newspaper articles as a classroom chum of Lyra's. Alice would make frequent visits to the Rhode Island homes of her fourth cousin, (Barbara) Harriet Talbot, the daughter of William Richmond Talbot of "Barberry Hill" in Warwick, Rhode Island and the Williams St. "Gaspee House" in Providence. The common ancestor of Alice and Harriet was (Daniel) Henry Gindrat of an aristocratic southern family.[9]

The Williams Street home was called the "Gaspee House" because paneling was salvaged from the Sabin Tavern (owned by the family of Harriet's mother, the Arnolds) on South Main Street to build an addition to the Williams Street house known as the Gaspee Room. It is said that the Sabin Tavern was the site of planning for the burning of the H.M.S. Gaspee. The Williams home became the headquarters of the Gaspee Chapter of the Daughters of the American Revolution. As a member of that Chapter, perhaps that is where Lyra became a close friend of Alice.

The burning of the Gaspee in 1772 was a harbinger of the American Revolution, preceding the Boston Tea Party by over a year. In response to the pillaging of Colonist ships in Narragansett Bay by the British, a group of colonists led by John Brown (co-founder of Brown University) boarded the Gaspee capturing the crew and then burning the Gaspee. "Gaspee Days" are celebrated each year in Pawtuxet Village to commemorate the event by burning a model of the ship.

The Montgomery Advertiser reported in October 1906 that Alice had just returned to Alabama after spending a year in Providence and Warwick. During the year, Alice had joined Lyra at several social gatherings in Rhode Island; e.g., a "Dainty Luncheon" given by Lyra in March for Miss Florence Hancock of Philadelphia.[10] In the summer of 1908, Alice spent a month with Lyra at Camp Wyongonic in East Denmark, Maine before returning to Barberry Hill for the month of September.

---

[9] Davis, Harry Alexander, *The Gindrat Family*, Washington, DC, 1933.
[10] Providence News, March 2, 1906.

The Debutante

Lyra's birthday, December 7th, was often celebrated with a lavish party. For example, when she turned nineteen in 1904, Lyra's parents hosted a tea to debut Lyra to Providence society. The Providence Journal reported that the beautiful interior of the Nickerson home *"together with the glory of flowers formed a picture not soon to be forgotten. The wall was banked with American Beauty roses, before which Mrs. Nickerson and Miss Nickerson received their guests. In every available space flowers bloomed, in baskets and bouquets, making the attractive reception rooms a scene of beauty. The centre of the richly carved table was adorned with orchids of purple with green foliage. The balustrade was entwined with a fine feathery green vine, while on the Newell post was artistically fastened a huge bunch of red carnations. Miss Nickerson was gowned in pure white, made charmingly simple and effective, white flowers completing a beautiful toilette."*[11] In contrast to her elite beginnings as a debutante, Lyra later became a champion of worthy causes in Providence, Rhode Island and the Nation.

Gilded Age Girls

The girls of Providence growing up on College Hill in the late 1800's became Lyra's close coterie of friends. From prominent East Side families; many attended Mrs. Spink's Dance Academy and Lincoln School with Lyra and, like Lyra, were prominent on the Society pages of the Providence newspapers.

Among Lyra's debutante contemporaries were the similarly alliterative pair Bonney Barry, the daughter of editor-in chief David S. Barry of the Providence Journal, and Beatrice Brown, the daughter of District Court Judge Arthur Lewis Brown. To compound the confusion about their names, Bonney went on to marry a Brown and Beatrice married a Berry. Lyra's other early gal pals included Lucy Cameron, Esther Tillinghast, Marguerite Cross, Elizabeth Hughes and the aforementioned Barbara Harriet Talbot.

---

[11] Providence Journal, *What is Doing in Local Society*, December 10, 1904, p. 10.

Noteworthy among the College Hill clique was Martha B. "Patty" Willson (Day), later achieving fame from her miniature portraits, Patty, like Lyra, was the daughter of a Providence architect -Edmund R. Willson. Willson was in the group of "Friday Knights" immortalized on the Art Club House Green Room table and silhouetted on its wall. Willson and artist Sydney Burleigh designed the unique Fleur de Lys studio of the Providence Art Club on Thomas Street. Patty lived at 88 Congdon Street in Providence, even after marriage to Howard Day and the birth of her two sons. Around 1930, Patty interviewed all the residents of Congden Street to document their thoughts and memories of living there and of the founding of Prospect Terrace, the site of the iconic Roger Williams statue and his final resting place. The Rhode Island Historical Society has archived the records of her work.

Hope C. Brown was the daughter of Rhode Island Governor D. Russell Brown. Hope married Howard M. Chapin, director of the Rhode Island Historical Society and a prolific author of Rhode Island historical books. The newlyweds boarded the *Carpathia* to head to Europe for their honeymoon, but their voyage was interrupted by a disaster at sea.

Helen Ostby attended Mrs. Spink's dance classes and Lincoln School with Lyra as well as attending many events hosted by Lyra. She achieved fame as a Titanic survivor.

8. *Helen Ostby*

Helen(e) Ostby was the daughter of the Engelhart Ostby, owner of Ostby and Barton Jewelers, and a 1909 College Hill debutante. She was returning from Europe on the Titanic and was separated from her father after the iceberg collision. She managed to board a lifeboat and was picked up by the *Carpathia*. Her friends, Mr. and Mrs. Howard Chapin (nee Hope Brown), took her in and allowed her to use their cabin. Engelhart went down with the ship. His body was recovered and buried in Swan Point Cemetery. Helen was a competitive tennis player and, like Lyra, was travelling in Germany at the outbreak of World War I. She escaped to Flanders only to have to the Germans invade neutral Belgium. Remarkably, she was living in Belgium at the start of hostilities in World War II. Helen never married and was buried next to her father at Swan Point in 1978.[12]

---

[12] Laxton, Glenn, *Hidden History of Rhode Island*, 2009, History Press, Charleston, SC, pp. 100-104.

2. The Heiress

The origin of the wealth and property of Lyra Brown Nickerson traces back to the Brown and Sharpe company and its founder and patriarch of the Brown family, Joseph Rogers Brown. Lyra was named as a major beneficiary of Brown and Sharpe stock, monies and real estate passed on by the Brown estate.

The Will of Joseph Rogers Brown

Joseph Brown willed the bulk of his estate, primarily stock in Brown and Sharpe, to be divided equally between his second wife Jane and in trust to his daughter with Caroline Nils, Lyra Frances, who had married Edward I. Nickerson. Trustees and executors of the will were Lucien Sharpe and Charles D. Owen, an owner of Atlantic Mills in the neighborhood of Olneyville in Providence. Olneyville had been named after Christopher Olney, who had built a grist mill and paper mill on the site. The trustees of Joseph's will were tasked to manage the trust and pay its income to Joseph's daughter periodically. With the approval of the court, they could also terminate the trust and convey the trust property to her and to her heirs.[13]

In lieu of title to his estate at 119 Congdon Street, Joseph's wife Jane F. Brown was given all of the house contents and lifetime occupancy and use of the house. As next of kin, his only surviving child, Lyra Frances, was entitled to ownership of the 119 Congdon Street house which was specified to be hers to have and to hold after the death of Jane.

The Wills of Lyra F. Nickerson and Edward I. Nickerson

When Lyra Frances passed away in 1907, ownership of 119 Congdon St. was given by her will to her stepmother, Jane F. Brown. The home on Angell Street and all of its contents went to her husband Edward and to her daughter Lyra after his death. The trust income from all of her stock in Brown and Sharpe was to be split evenly between Edward during his life and daughter Lyra. Her wish was that, "under certain contingencies, after the deaths of her husband and daughter, gifts of considerable size" would be given to the Providence Public Library and the Rhode Island School of Design (RISD). After the death of Edward, when daughter Lyra reached age 30, the trust was to be terminated, and the stock would be given to her. One "certain

---

[13] Providence Journal, *The Will of Joseph R. Brown*, Aug. 2, 1876, p.2.

contingency" was that, if daughter Lyra was without will and heirs, proceeds from the stock would be split between the Library and RISD.

Edward I. Nickerson died in 1908, the following year. With the exception of properties on Pine Street to the three sons of his sister Elizabeth Williams and some other specific bequests, his entire estate was given to Lyra Brown Nickerson.

The Art Treasures of Edward I. Nickerson

Edward Irving Nickerson was not only a prominent Rhode Island architect, but he also was a student of the craft and maintained a large number of books on the subject. His extensive travels in Europe, South America and northern Africa, sometimes accompanied by his daughter Lyra, allowed him to amass a collection of precious works of art. The Rhode Island School of Design commented *"She toured with her father throughout Europe, and these trips were perhaps where she also came into contact with objects now in our collection. Her bequeathed gifts include artworks and objects from a range of countries, including Bolivia, Algeria, South Africa, Sweden, Italy, Egypt, and Japan."*[14] The Nickersons were on board for this sail:

Imperial German and U. S. Mail Steamship

HOHENZOLLERN.
W. MEISSEL, Commander.

Sailing from New York for Genoa via Gibraltar and Naples,

SATURDAY, JUNE 6th, 1903.

The items below are examples from Edward I. Nickerson's collection, now at the Rhode Island. School of Design.

9. Egyptian Canopic Jar

10. Italian Slippers

---

[14] Digitalcommons.risd.edu, Fall 2020, Issue 14, *Shadows*.

Lyra donated her father's complete architectural library consisting of seven hundred volumes to the Providence Public Library in addition to a $10,000 endowment whose earnings were used to update the collection. Titles by Vitruvius, Palladio, Inigo Jones, and Piranesi are included in the Nickerson Art and Architecture Collection. Vitruvius lived in Rome toward the end of the 1st century BC. His treatise *On Architecture* has been used by architects throughout the ages. Andrea Palladio (1508-1580) was considered the greatest northern Italian Renaissance architect of the 16th century. His villas and palaces are examples of a style that was widely copied in future years. He authored a set of four books about architecture describing the so-called Palladian methods. Inigo Jones (1573-1652), an English Renaissance architect, followed the Palladian style and is noted for his designing the Banquet Hall at Whitehall Palace in London. Giovanni Battista Piranesi (1720-1778) was an architect remembered principally for his detailed etchings such as the *Round Tower*.

11. Piranesi Etching[15]

---

[15] National Gallery of Art, Giovanni Bouchard, *Carceri d'invenzione*.\, 1981.8.

The Will of Jane Frances Brown

When Joseph's widow, Jane (Mowry) Brown, passed away at age 90, she left all of her shares of Brown and Sharpe stock specifically to the sons of Lucien Sharpe and to others associated with the business. The pecuniary part of her estate was divided and included $200,000 to Rhode Island Hospital for what became the Jane Brown Hospital addition.

12. The Jane Brown Hospital[16]

Other large bequests were $200,000 to Grace Episcopal Church in Providence, $300,000 to St. Paul's Church in Pawtucket and $25,000 to St. Joseph's Hospital. Mrs. Brown willed pew #103 at the Grace Church to John T. Cranshaw. Until 1920, parishioners could own or rent a pew at the church. A trust fund in the amount of $100,000 was to be given to Rev. William M. Chapin of Barrington and his heirs. Granddaughter Jane Brown Jones was bequeathed $100,000. Several more individual bequests were listed to make the total pecuniary legacies in the will to be $1,163,000. All the remaining part of the estate was to be given to granddaughter Lyra Brown Nickerson. However, Jane Brown had given away much of her fortune during her lifetime, so the assets of her estate, other than her stocks and home on Congdon Street, amounted to about $890,000, not even enough to cover the monetary bequests. Contrary to early reports, Lyra received little or nothing from Jane Brown's estate.

A notable specific bequest by Jane Brown was to her long-time nurse, cited as Miss Ellen Logan, who was described as "youthful and pretty." Miss Logan was given the Brown mansion on Congdon Street with all the home furnishings in addition to $100,000.[17] It was the largest

---

[16] Photograph by Clive Nickerson.
[17] Boston Globe, 3 Aug 1913, p. 1.

gift ever given by a patient to her nurse in Rhode Island. When told of her huge inheritance, the nurse "swooned" and had to be hospitalized. It seems that Jane Brown was not particularly good with names as Ellen Logan was, in truth, Mary Christina Logan. The 1920 Rhode Island census recorded Margaret Logan and her daughters, including Mary Christina, living at the Congdon Street house. The whole family had "moved on up" from Smith Hill to College Hill. Mary Christina Logan lived there till the end of her life in 1963.

Lyra Brown Nickerson, born in 1885, being the only child was the sole natural heir of the Lyra Frances and Edward Irving Nickerson estates. At the tender age of 22 in 1908, Lyra had lost both of her parents within the current and previous year. Upon the death of both her parents, Lyra inherited a legacy from Joseph Rogers Brown, founder of Brown and Sharpe, in the amount of $6,000,000 which is nearly $180,000,000 in 2024 dollars.

The trust that had been established for Lyra after the death of her mother was terminated on her 30th birthday, December 7, 1915, and the shares of Brown and Sharpe stock therein were given to Lyra to keep or sell as she wished. Her mother's will stipulated that it should first be offered back to Brown and Sharpe.

Joseph Brown and his two wives, Caroline and Jane, were buried together in Swan Point Cemetery, marked by a tetrahedral stone with their names respectively inscribed on the three visible faces of the stone The graves of the Nickerson family members are nearby.

13. Browns Headstone

Saving Angell Street

Lyra continued to live on Angell Street and retained the family's Irish servants, Alice Curry and Margaret Johnston. According to the 1910 census, Lyra's second cousin, Jane Brown Jones, age 70, was also living at the Angell Street address.

A few years after losing her parents, Lyra was in danger of losing her home. On what is known as College Hill, 19th century trolley transportation from the city required a counterweight cable system to negotiate the $10°$ to $15°$ incline by hoisting the cars up the hill. In 1911, a commission was formed to design an alternate system. Construction of a road through College Hill was proposed by commission member John R. Freeman, a noted civil engineer who had designed the Charles River Dam, part of the Panama Canal, as well as many other significant and substantial engineering projects. The proposal to replace the cable system included cutting a new road called Roger Williams Street that would run obliquely through Lyra's neighborhood, reducing the incline sufficiently to eliminate the need for the counterweight system. Lyra wrote a letter to the Providence Journal in 1911 strongly objecting to that idea that would decimate houses on Angell Street, including No. 71, Lyra's home.

14. John R. Freeman

The Freeman Plan called for moving Lyra's home out of the path of the new road and demolishing another house at 52 Angell Street which belonged to Lyra.

The Freeman commission report claimed that the "mansions at the corner of Prospect Street and Angell Street would be benefited rather than injured, for the squealing and grinding of the street cars would be removed and the cars would pass at so low a level that their noises would hardly be so serious as now, although the traffic would more than double." [19]

A public hearing was held about the issue. The description in The Journal was colorful.[18] *"The verbiage was profuse. The defendant's plan, which was seized and exhibited, was declared to be a monstrosity, a crime, a blot, a monumental mistake, a horror, a desecration, a tunnel with the roof off, a ragged obstruction, a gash, an eyesore, a sluice, an abomination, and a number of other things."* The proceedings were often interrupted by cheers from the residents of Angell Street.

The Nickerson family lawyer, Richard B. Comstock, spoke for Lyra Brown Nickerson. "Miss Nickerson," he said, "is as ready and willing as any citizen of Providence to make sacrifices for the common good, but is not willing to give up her home and property for an object that is going to prove a disadvantage instead of an advantage. We can't improve God's work and we can't improve that hill. Why can't we have a tunnel?"

State Representative Theodore Francis Green, who later became the oldest U.S. Senator at age 93, voiced his objection to the Freeman Plan. Mr. Green's primary concern was the desecration of a Providence landmark, the First Baptist Meeting House Church on Benefit Street. The plan would require cutting into the Church property within 15 feet of the Church itself. "One of the chief objects of interest to Providence is the First Baptist Church. Take away the setting, the lawn, the trees and the grass, and the loss cannot be estimated," said Representative Green. He added, "The First Baptist Church building is the greatest piece of Colonial architecture in the United States, and any proposition to destroy it makes us who have always lived here hot under the collar." [19]

---

[18] Providence Daily Journal, *Freeman Proposal Bitterly Assailed,* April 14, 1911, p.1.

[19] Theusgenweb.org, *History of the State of Rhode Island and Providence Plantations: Biographical,* NY: The American Historical Society, Inc. 1920.

15. Theodore Francis Green

    The solution that the electric trolley company ultimately decided upon was construction of a tunnel from North Main Street to Thayer Street, replacing the cumbersome counterweight system. In 1913, Lyra granted an easement to the 63 Angell Street property with regard to construction of the Thayer Street stretch of the tunnel. The question became moot in future years because the widespread use of automobiles allowed access to College Hill without the need of trolleys. The tunnel was eventually used just for bus traffic.

Richard B Comstock

Attorney Richard Borden Comstock represented Lyra at the hearings. His distinguished career later included serving as president of the Rhode Island Bar Association. He lived on Humboldt Ave. in the East Side of Providence with his wife Alice and three daughters Marjorie, Louise and Alice who were Lyra's contemporaries. The family spent their summers in Little Compton, RI where Richard became a founder of the Sakonnet Golf Club. Richard and Alice were prominent members of the Club and of the seasonal community. Their daughters even formed a theater troupe to produce and star in plays for the entertainment of summer residents.

Richard often represented the elite of Newport. One famous client was John Jacob Astor IV, who was seeking a preacher willing to perform the marriage between the divorced 47-year-old Astor to 18-year-old socialite Madeleine Talmage Force. Comstock was acting as Astor's "Cupid" in this difficult quest as almost all Rhode Island ministers wanted no part of this scandal. Richard nearly resorted to selecting a 70-year-old carpenter who had retired as a Baptist minister 30 years prior. The Reverend Joseph Lambert of Providence's Elmwood Temple Congregational Church ultimately agreed to perform the ceremony but afterwards promptly resigned his ministry under a barrage of criticism. The socialist Industrial Worker[20] newspaper reported that Lambert resigned in shame for marrying "...Aster to some little girl in short dresses." for a fee of possibly $20,000 or more. The following year, the vacationing Astors boarded the maiden voyage of the *Titantic*, so that the pregnant Madeleine would give birth in the United States. John Jacob Astor IV famously perished along with over 1500 others while Madeleine was rescued by the *Carpathia* and went on the marry twice more.

---

[20] *Industrial Worker*, Vol. 3, Issue 36, Spokane, WA., Nov. 30, 1911.

PART II: Lyra The Woman

1. The Socialite

The multi-millionaire heiress Lyra became one of the most prominent personalities in Providence. She could well have been called "The Princess of Providence" for her position in the elite society of the city. Like many of the wealthy in her generation, she enjoyed the lifestyle of the rich and famous; but, at the same time, felt that it was her life's mission to promote the welfare of those in need.

The Princess of Providence

The annual subscription dance for Misses Bowen and Gilman's Lincoln School was held in 1904 at the Casino in Providence's Roger Williams Park. About 150 attended, Lyra and the other young women there being former pupils at the school. The men were eligible bachelors from Providence society and Brown University. Lyra's friends Beatrice Brown and Lucy Cameron organized the event with the helpful patronage of their mothers. One of the college boys attending was young Zechariah Chafee, Jr. "Zach" was the grandson of Lucien Sharpe Sr. and later became the uncle of Governor John Chafee and granduncle of Governor Lincoln Chafee. Zechariah in later life was a noted civil libertarian and author. Miss Bowen's retirement in June of 1906 was cause for a luncheon attended by Lyra, Lucy, and Bonney Barry. [21]

Another notable attendee of the Bowen luncheon was (Mary) Louise Lippitt, daughter of U. S. Senator Henry F. Lippitt. The aristocratic Lippitt family are prominent in the history of Rhode Island and Providence in particular. Both Henry's father and his brother served as Rhode Island governors. In October 1908, Louise married Philadelphian George Sinnickson in the Lippitt family home on Benefit Street on College Hill.[22]

In January of 1906, the annual "Gymnasium Ball" was held at the Brown University's Lyman Gym. This affair was the most selective and exclusive of Providence's social season. Twenty-year old Lyra Brown Nickerson was invited along with her College Hill friends Beatrice Brown and Bonney Barry from Washington, D.C.

---

[21] Providence News-Democrat, June 15, 1906.
[22] Philadelphia Inquirer, Oct. 20, 1908, p.7.

The committee for the annual Lincoln School dance in 1907 was chaired by Lyra. The event was again attended by Beatrice Brown, Lucy Cameron and Zechariah Chafee, Jr. Among the young men attending was Henry Garfield Clark, Lyra's future fiancé.[23] Also in attendance was E. Tudor Gross, who later competed, as did Mrs. Gross, in the Pinehurst, NC mid-winter tennis competitions. Lyra joined Tudor and his wife, the former Louise Windsor Hunt, at Pinehurst to enter the competitions herself. Louise had been the 1906 Rhode Island women's golf champion.

A costume ball was held by the Rhode Island School of Design in May of 1907. Both Lyra and Theodore Francis Green came in Turkish attire.[24]

Lyra was famous for her lavish "entertainments." She hosted several events that became "must attend" happenings for the affluent of Providence's East Side. One such affair was a reception and dance held at Churchill House on Angell Street. Churchill House had been founded in 1907 as a women's center and became a focal point for women's suffrage. The occasion for the event was Lyra's 25th birthday. It was described by the Providence Journal as the most brilliant event of the social season thus far. *"The crowning effect came as a surprise just before midnight, when the dancing was in progress. Suddenly the lights were lowered, and from the balcony rail, where it was skillfully surrounded by wreaths of laurel, was a soft gleam of electric lights in the dates '1885, DEC. 7, 1910' the birthday date of the hostess, who received many congratulations on the spot."*[25]

Lyra held a "Ladies Afternoon" of music at the Providence Art Club in January 1914. Lyra, Marguarite Cross Edgren, Hope Brown Chapin, Patty Willson and Cecilia Lacey-Baker served tea.[26] Lyra's events dominated the Society page of the Sunday Journal in September 1914. Notices of the upcoming "Tennis Ball" (see below), Federal Hill House subscription dance, a visit to her home by Conway Evans, and a first anniversary dinner for the Urban Edgrens (Marguarite Cross) hosted by Lyra were all mentioned.[27]

A most elegant floral party was given for Lyra prior to her tour of South America where she was to be guided by Mrs. Conway Evans. Mrs. Evans played a key role in the adventure described in Chapter 3,

---

[23] Providence News-Democrat, May 31, 1907.

[24] Providence News-Democrat, May 1907.

[25] Providence Journal, *Reception and Dance, Brilliant Affair Given by Miss Nickerson* Dec. 7, 1910, p.11,

[26] Providence Evening News, Jan 15, 1914.

[27] Providence Sunday Journal, Sept 24, 1914.

The Spy. Conway was a noted traveler and lecturer about faraway lands. She was born in British Guiana as Louisa Conway Pitman, the daughter of sugar plantation owner Augustus James Pitman. Conway later married Edward Evans and decided to be known as Mrs. Conway Evans from then on.

A Rose Ball Farewell

Providence, R. I., has had a ball of great degree. It was a farewell for Miss Lyra Brown Nickerson, given on the eve of her departure for a three-month tour of South America, and attended by between 400 and 500 men and women of society of her home city and state, with many guests from distant cities. The lower floor of the building was turned into a Spanish garden, and a most elaborate one.

In the southwest corner Miss Nickerson received with Mrs. Conway Evans in a bower of green, with an overhead canopy of green. Hundreds of pink roses surrounded the bower, creating a wonderful effect of pink and green. Miss Nickerson wore a gown of filmy cream lace and crystal over a foundation of yellow satin with girdle and sash of pale blue.

A seated supper was a feature, and during its six courses a troubador sang. Other novel features were the entrance of a Scotch bag piper and two dancers, who marched around the room in a fancy dance to the music of the bagpipes, and just before supper was served a shower of rose leaves fell over the entire assembly, marking the collapse of four huge roses hanging from the ceiling of the ballroom.

The above is a colorful description of the "Rose Ball" that appeared in the Washington Evening Star on 21 January 1915. Such balls attended by hundreds of prominent members of society were typical for Lyra's social agenda.

On October 31, 1914, Miss Nickerson held a "Tennis Ball" to celebrate the official opening of her new tennis court. A tennis match began the evening's events with E. Tudor Gross pitted against his nemesis, state champion J.D.E. Jones. Jones won in straight sets and was presented with a loving cup by Lyra. A buffet and dancing followed the match with music provided by an orchestra. In 1915, Lyra hosted a number of *Thes Dansants* (afternoon tea dances) at the tennis court.

Lyra had hosted tea dances in 1913 and 1914[28], notably presented by the outstanding ballroom dance doyenne of the era, Margaret Hawkesworth, at Churchill House and Froebel Hall (later to become Hillel Hall servicing the Jewish community) on the corner of Angell and Brown Street. Margaret and her partner were Lyra's Angell Street guests.

16. Margeret Hawkesworth and Partner[29]

---

[28] Providence Evening News, May 1913 and January 1914.

Narragansett Pier

Lyra spent her summers at a leased villa at Kentara Green, a complex of cottages at Narragansett Pier on the Bay. Kentara Green was situated off Gibson Street in Narragansett and consisted of a main casino and restaurant bracketed by three cottages on either side. It was built by famed New York restauranteur Louis Sherry whose eponymous establishment catered to the elites in the City.

17. Kentara Green[29]

She was the hostess of many gala events at the Pier such as clambakes attended by the other affluent summer residents. In 1912, a fire destroyed several of the cottages, but Lyra's was spared. A group of polo players had climbed to the roof of Lyra's residence and covered it with wet blankets and sheets, saving it from catching fire.[30]
New York Times reported (July 28, 1912):
"Miss Lyra Nicholson (sic), who occupied Viewfield in the Kentara group, sped to fire in a motor car, clad in a bathing suit. Many other cottagers went from the beach to the fire in bathing suits."

One year later on July 5, 1913, another fire at Narragansett Pier gutted the Presbyterian church. Nearby cottages were saved thanks to a donation by Lyra.

---

[29] independentri.com, *Garage Under Construction at Kentara Green,* Stephen. Greenwell, Jr., photo courtesy of Sallie Latimer, May 9, 2015.

[30] *Philadelphia Inquirer*, (PA), 28 Jul 1912.

From the Times:
"Quick work with the chemical engine, which was provided to the town by Miss Lyra Brown Nickerson, prevented a disastrous fire."

Below is a current photo of one of "cottages" or villas as they were known.[31]

18. Kentara Cottage

---

[31] *The Independent*, Narragansett, RI, Michael Dorr, staff photographer.

'Immigrant' Ball

While at Narragansett in 1915, Lyra received the following invitation to the Scarborough Beach Club:

United States of America, Bureau of Immigration

This is to certify that Lyra Brown Nickerson is entitled to life, liberty and the pursuit of happiness at the Scarbor<u>ellis</u> <u>Island</u> Club on the evening of Saturday, August 7.
N.B.---The boat docks at 10 o'clock
    Mr. and Mrs Rowland Hazard
    Mr. and Mrs. S. H. Bird
U. S. Commisioners of Immigration

Guests were instructed to wear immigrant "habiliments" rather than their usual beach clothes and the guests complied with colorful garb. Also invited to the Ball were profesional dancers Lucia Chase and Anoinette Bloodgood who were starring in the operettta "Gay Revillin" at the Narraganseett Pier Casino.

19. Lucia Chase and Antoinette Bloodgood

Later in August, the annual costume ball was held at the Casino. Lucia and Antoinette wore a peasant dress and a "Tommy Atkins" (British soldier) uniform, respectively. The outfits were likely what they also had worn to the "Immigrant" Ball.

Lucia was a summer resident of Narragansett with her parents, Irving H. and Elizabeth (Hosmer) Chase and her sisters at their estate "Miramar" on Ocean Road. "Miramar" was built in 1900 on the site of Narragansett House, the Pier's first hotel.

Kitty Schermerhorn

Another cottage at Kentara Green was occupied in the summer by the Jacob Maus Schermerhorn family. Young Katherine "Kitty" Schermerhorn was a close friend of Lyra's. The European "arresting" adventure of Kitty, Mrs. Conway Evans and Lyra is described in Chapter 3, The Spy.

Kitty Schermerhorn was born in Providence in 1893 as Katherine Thomas Browne, the 7th child of Keyes Danforth Browne and Bertha Thomas Burt. After the death of her mother in 1910, Katherine at age 16 went to live with her childless aunt, Mary Bushnell Browne, age 58, and her husband industrialist Jacob Schermerhorn, age 63. The Schermerhorns adopted her and she took their name. After spending years living in Manhattan while renting a summer cottage at Kentara Green, the Schermerhorns moved back to Providence. The year 1916 was a sad one for Kitty, as her adoptive mother died and she lost her close friend.

Kitty Schermerhorn was a guest at many of Lyra's "entertainments," both in Narragansett and in Providence. The "Tennis Ball" in the East Providence Indoor Court was co-hosted by Kitty and Lyra. Lyra's Narragansett clambakes and dinners were ususally attended by Kitty. Perhaps only child Lyra thought of her as a younger sister. Katherine was also a frequent travelling companion of Lyra's. She later married Mauran Seagrave Pearce. Kitty passed away in 1987 and was buried in Swan Point Cemetery with her husband and adoptive parents as were many affluent East Side residents.

Weddings

Lyra's social life extended well beyond Rhode Island. She often visited her friend Alice Lahey in Montgomery, Alabama and became the maid of honor at Alice's wedding to James Henry Foster.

Lyra was in demand to be part of society's wedding scene. Notably, she was a bridesmaid for the nuptual union of two prominent publishing families. Lyra was a bridesmaid for Elizabeth Bonney Barry, daughter of David S. Barry, editor-in-chief of the Providence Journal, when she married Sevellon Ledyard Brown, successor to David Barry as editor and eventually publisher of the Journal. Lyra served as maid of honor in 1909 at the wedding of Lucy Cameron to Norman Sammis, Brown '07, in Philadelphia. She was also in the wedding party of Beatrice Brown, who married Harold H. Berry at the Grace Epispocal Church in Providence. [32]

Elizabeth Hughes was the granddaughter of Thomas H. Hughes, founder of the Hughesdale Dye and Chemical Works in the eponymous Hughesdale Village of Johnston, Rhode Island. The Hughes family were all parishioners at Providence's Grace Episcopal Church. After the death of her father William H. Hughes at the turn of the century, Elizabeth and her mother Eliza (Atwood) Hughes moved in with her aunt, Elizabeth (Atwood) Dyer on Benefit Street in Providence. Her mother Eliza passed away in 1907. On June 3, 1912, Elizabeth exchanged marriage vows with Arthur Chester Snow at the Hughesdale homestead Stone Acres. Maid of Honor Lyra Brown Nickerson wore a *"rose voile gown, pannier effect, with ecru lace bandeau of pink maline ornamented with a bird of paradise."*[33] Another friend from College Hill, Esther Tillinghast, was a bridesmaid and Grace Church Rector Ralph Crowder performed the ceremony. Theodore Hughes, who had taken over the business after his father's death, gave the bride away. Sadly, Elizabeth succumbed to chronic nephritis less than seventeen months after taking her marriage vows. Lyra lost her College Hill friend Elizabeth in October of 1913.

The Tennis Court

In 1913, Lyra purchased land for the Indoor Tennis Court on Blanding Street in East Providence, Rhode Island for only $100. Later that year, construction began and was completed with $20,000 contributed by Lyra. An avid tennis competitor herself, Lyra hosted many famous top-ranked players including Norwegian phenom Molla Bjurstedt. Tennis legend Bill Tilden later trained and played on her court where he perfected his backhand. The Indoor Court was also used for Lyra's lavish parties.[34]

Lyra, as a tennis player, competed in the mid-winter Pinehurst, NC competition as did several other Providence and Agawam Hunt Club entries. She advanced to the second round in women's doubles and mixed doubles but was knocked out in the first round of singles. Her

---

[32] Birmingham (AL) Age-Herald, March 15, 1916 p. 6.

[33] Providence Evening News, June 4, 1912.

[34] Brun, Tom, "The Indoor Tennis Court and Miss Lyra Brown Nickerson", *Senior Tennis 2008*, pp. 3-7.

friends E. Tudor Gross and Mrs. Gross also were competitors at Pinehurst. Mrs. Gross lost her first round singles match but her husband advanced to the third round of men's singles and the second round of men's doubles.[35]

20. Bill Tilden[36]

      The Indoor Court attracted the very best players in the nation. Foremost among them was Anna Margarethe Bjurstedt, better known as Molla. The US Open website has referred to Molla as "The Greatest Champion You Have Never Heard Of." In 1916, she was rated the top woman's tennis player in the world, having won the U.S Open and the indoor tennis championship. Molla went on to win seven more U.S. titles, setting an American record that still stands. She has a place of honor in Court of Champions at the Billie Jean King National Tennis Center alongside Billie Jean, Chris Evert and Martina Navratilova. Molla also won three U. S. Open mixed doubles including two with Bill Tilden, a "dream team" if there ever was one. She was a house guest of Lyra along with indoor tennis champion Marie Wagner and Florence Ballin, who had partnered with Molla in the Open doubles and Bill Tilden in the Open mixed doubles finals. While staying with Lyra the women participated in exhibition matches at the Indoor Court.[37]

---

[35] Pinehurst Outlook, Pinehurst, NC, Feb. 5, 1916, pp. 13-14.
[36] https://www.db4tennis.com/players/male/william-tilden-ii.
[37] Providence Journal, April 2, 1916.

Molla was quoted as saying "I believe in hitting the ball with all my might." Billie Jean King called her "a thunderous backcourt player." Molla was again a house guest at Lyra's cottage on Kentara Green in Narragansett in August 1916 when she played an exhibition match against male opponent "Harry" P. Cross at the RI championship held at he Agawam Hunt Club. He was defeated in straight sets with Molla's aggressive style. He suffered from exhaustion from the fast pace and had to be helped off the court under the adverse heat conditions.[38] Molla was challenged again by a male opponent when at the Newport Casino. She defeated Oliver Perrin to decide a bet as to whether male or females were better players. Molla bet on herself and won in straight sets. Billie Jean King followed in her footsteps in 1973 by famously defeating Bobby Riggs in a match that was dubbed "The Battle of the Sexes."

Lyra gave a dinner in honor of Molla at the Narragansett Pier Casino on August 6, 1916. Among the guests was Lyra's fiancé, Henry Clark. It was one of several summer soirees that Lyra hosted or attended in a short period of time that year. Molla was notorious for puffing cigarettes before, after and during matches. She was quoted as saying *"It clears away the air and helps me breathe."*

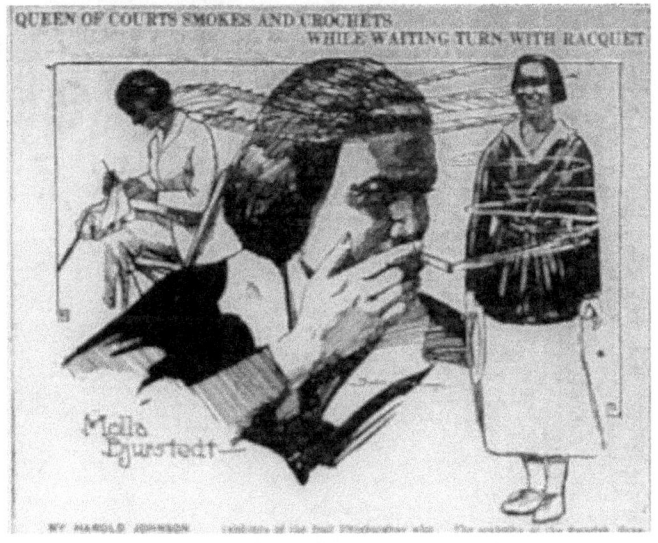

21. *Smoking Molla*[39].

---

[38] Providence Journal, August 8, 1916.

[39] The Seattle Star, July 7, 1916.

"I find that the girls generally do not hit the ball as hard as they should. I believe in always hitting the ball with all my might, but there seems to be a disposition to 'just get it over' in many girls whom I have played. I do not call this tennis."[40] --Molla Bjurstedt

Lyra also welcomed R. Norris Williams II, the top ranked male tennis champion, who had the distinction of being a Titanic survivor. James Cameron used his story in his award-winning movie about the disaster. Williams was not the only Titanic passenger to be in Lyra's life. Lyra also had as a guest at many her parties (including the fete for Molla) Rhode Islander and Titantic survivor Helen Ostby.

---

[40] Encyclopedia.com, Molla Mallory entry.

Black and White Balls

"Black and White" masquerade balls were all the rage in Rhode Island including those held at the Narragansett Pier Casino in July and August of 1915. Ballrooms were decked in black and white décor and guests were instructed to dress solely in black and white. The climax of the July event was when Antoinette Bloodgood opened a hanging black birdcage to release four white doves and a multitude of white rose petals. The petals were showered on the guests but the doves would not leave their roosts. A birdcage themed event was held later in August in Newport to honor Rhode Island Governor Beeckman. The governor's table was decorated to resemble a birdcage complete with live doves, canaries and thrushes.

Later in the year, another such "Black and White" event for the benefit of the Providence Day Nursery Association (later to become the Nickerson House) was hosted by Lyra and her fiancé Henry Clark at the Infantry Hall in Providence and was crowded to capacity of 2000 seated and many standing observers. James Reese Europe and his "colored" band provided the music for what was described as the event of the season. The hosts were dressed in costumes resembling the iconic Pierrot and Pierette clown/mime characters. Lyra wore *"an exceedingly becoming costume of white satin with black points, white Tam-o'Shanter cap with black pompom and white ruche. Mr. Clark's costume was its counterpoint, reversing the colors, black, predominating."* The costume judges included Rhode Island Governor Beeckman and Providence Mayor Gainer. Beatrice Brown Berry won the women's cup wearing an outfit very similar to Lyra's.[41]

Truman Capote resurrected the Black and White Ball in 1966 by throwing what was described as the "party of the century." He invited 450 of his "closest friends" –everybody who was anybody—to the Plaza Hotel in New York for his gala. The premier luminaries from entertainment, the arts, politics, jounalism, business, royalty, politics and the social scene were all there.[42]

---

[41] Providence Sunday Journal, *Black and White Ball*, November 28, 1915, p.3.
[42] Town and Country Magazine, *The True Story of Truman Capote's Black and White Ball*, Feb. 9, 2024.

Lyra brought the ball to her classmate Alice Lahey Foster in Alabama. Here is Lyra in full costume. [43]

22. Black and White Lyra

MISS LYRA BROWN NICKERSON, of Providence, R.I., the lovely guest of Mrs. Henry Foster, whose costume was one of the most attractive and unique worn at the Black and White ball last Tuesday evening at the Southern club. Miss Nickerson wore this costume when she recently led a black and white ball in Providence.

After the masquerade ball, Lyra's party moved on to Mardi Gras in New Orleans. Their visit was also noted in the Birmingham Age Herald as Lyra hosted another party.

---

[43] Birmingham (AL) Age-Herald, March 5, 1916, Editorial Section Image 25 from Chroniclingamerica.

BIRMINGHAM PEOPLE IN NEW ORLEANS

Miss Lyra Nickerson will be remembered as the recent guest of Mr. and Mrs. Henry Foster in this city, having been present at the black and white ball.

Says the New Orleans Item: In another party at the Louisiane Monday night was Miss Lira Nickerson of Providence. A young woman of great wealth, it is her sweet pleasure to give pleasure to her friends and to generously let them in on her good times. So she was here as the hostess of a party consisting of Captain and Mrs. Screws of Montgomery and of Mr. and Mrs. Henry Foster of Birmingham. Mrs. Foster and Mrs. Screws are sisters, you see, and both old friends of Miss Nickerson.

I think the party "did" carnival thoroughly and well, from their arrival on Sunday until Wednesday, when the hostess sailed for New York, the Fosters and Captain Screws departed on the train, and Mrs. Screws "moved" from the Grunewald up to Mrs. Lucien Lyons for a short visit.

The Lacey-Bakers

Lyra had also visited the Laheys in Alabama in late 1912, that time accompanied by Cecilia Lacey-Baker. While in the South, Lyra and Cecilia ventured to Florida and Cuba for several weeks with Mrs. Joseph Holt (Lucile Lahey). Cecilia was the daughter of Arthur Lacey-Baker, internationally known English musician and composer of liturgical themes who served as organist and choir director of the Grace Memorial Church in Providence from 1910-1916.[44] The Lacey-Bakers lived on George St. near Brown University during this time.

In December 1914, while Arthur Lacey-Baker led the choir and congregation in the singing of "My Country Tis of Thee," Lyra presented gifts of an American and Rhode Island flag to Grace Church.[45]

Cecilia's mother, Emma Clementi Smith, was the granddaughter of illustrious composer and pianist Muzio Clementi.[46] Muzio was called "the father of the piano(forte)" for his innovations in the legato playing style and his piano designs. Muzio competed in a piano duel with Wolfgang Amadeus Mozart in December 1781 sponsored by Holy Roman Emperor Joseph II. The Emperor called it a draw and awarded each 50 ducats. A few weeks later, Mozart criticized Clementi, saying he didn't have "…worth of taste or feeling, in a word, a mere mechanic."

Lyra and Cecilia were travel companions on many trips . In December 1912 they spent some time in Atlantic City with Mrs. Howard Chapin (Hope Brown) and in October 1913 went on an extended trip to the Berkshires and Lake Mohawk with Mrs. Charles Hawkesworth (dancer Margaret's mother).

Cecilia Lacey-Baker and Mrs. Hawkesworth were Lyra's guests at Kentara Green in the summer of 1913. In July, Lyra and Cecilia attended a performance of "Pygmalion and Galatea" at the Mathewson Hotel on Narragansett Pier. Cecila's sister Marjorie played the lead role of Galatea.

Marjorie (aka Marjory) Lacey-Baker was a playwright, director and actor. She appeared in Cape Cod's Provincetown Players productions with a troupe that included poet Edna St. Vincent Millay.

---

[44] Gracechurchprovidence.org/music-at-grace.
[45] Providence Journal Dec. 21, 1914.
[46] London remembers.com/Percival Clementi Smith.

23. Marjorie Lacey-Baker (center)

Majorie had a 36-year relationship with Lena Madesin Phillips, founder and president of The National Business and Professional Women's Clubs. She described Lena as "the woman with whom I share my home".[48] For her part, Cecilia became engaged to Theodore Grayson in 1911 but married Harold M. Pitman at Grace Church In October of 1914. Paul C. Nickerson (not a close relative of Lyra) was best man.

Lyra planned to sail to Europe on the gigantic German steamer *Vaterland* of the Hamburg America Line in the summer of 1914 with Arthur and Cecilia Lacey-Baker; however, the *Vaterland* never left New York because of the hostilities in Europe. The ship stayed in port for three years and was seized by the U. S. for military transportation and later renamed the *Leviathan* as a passenger ship.

Arthur and Cecilia sailed for Italy in mid-June 1914 on Hamburg America ship, the *Cleveland*. Lyra and Katherine Schermerhorn had made it to Europe on another giant boat, Hamburg America's *Imperator* in May; but who, unknowingly, were about to have the adventure of their lives (see Chapter 3).

---

[47] Picryl.com//media// William Zorach and others.
[48] Wikipedia/wiki/Lena Madesin Phillips.

24. The Imperator

2. The Philanthropist

Throughout her life, without fanfare, Lyra responded to the needs of many charitable and educational causes. In 1912, she had made a $7000 contribution to the Brown University endowment fund which was later used to provide fellowships for needy students. That year she also conducted a sale at Froebel Hall for the benefit of St. Mary's Episcopal Orphanage in East Providence. Lyra also contributed $1000 to reconstruction of a wing of the RI Historical Society to make it fire proof, but the paramount lasting example of Lyra's generosity to those less fortunate was her gift to establish the "Nickerson House."

The Nickerson Settlement House

The origin of the Nickerson House can be traced back to actions by the Grace Episcopal Church in Providence. The Reverend David H. Greer, Rector of Grace Church from 1872 to 1888, headed up a committee to establish a care center for young children of mill working women. The location established was the Grace Memorial Home which had been designed by church member Edward I. Nickerson, Lyra's father. The Home became the primary site of the Providence Day Nursery Association.

25. *Grace Memorial Home*

The location of the Grace Memorial Home was on Delaine Street in Olneyville Village in close proximity to the Atlantic and other local textile mills. Working mothers from largely Italian and Polish immigrant families in the neighborhood conveniently dropped off their children for

---

[49] Providence Journal, 6th Section, *A Many-In-One Philanthropic Centre*, May 13, 1917.

day care as they went to work in the mills. The needs of children ranging in age from three months old to 10 years were provided, including meals, recreation and general care.

As programs were added and utilization of the Home increased, more space was required. In 1915, Lyra Brown Nickerson contributed $20,000 to the Providence Day Nursery Association for construction of an additional building on the corner of Delaine and Appleton Streets.

26. The Nickerson House[50]

The Association provided Providence's first community health service in the building which was later named in honor of their benefactor Lyra. Near the entrance, there was a large room seating 275 including a stage that was utilized for social welfare meetings. The basement was well-lighted and was used as a playroom.[51]

27. Nickerson House Playroom

---

[50] Providence Public Library Digital Collections, Cady, p. 267.

[51] Rhode Island Historical Society, Manuscripts Division, Nickerson House Records, 1884-2001, Cat. MSS 1122, Rick Stratton, July 2003.

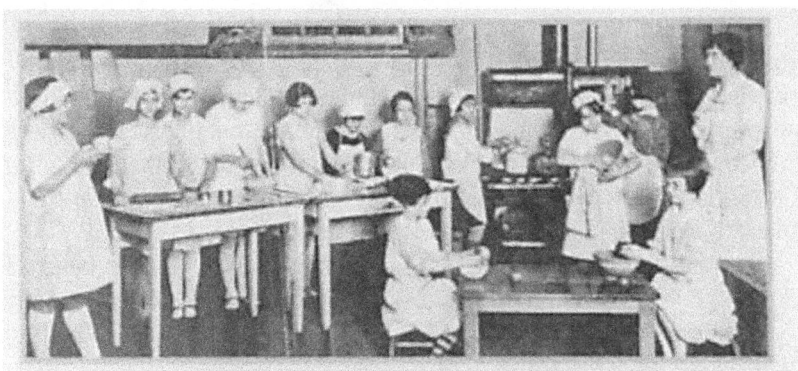
28. Cooking Class

The Home included a "modern" kitchen with up-to-date appliances where children studied "domestic science." The upstairs rooms housed eye, throat and dental clinics. A clinic for the diagnosis and treatment of tuberculosis was opened. There was even a milk station on the Appleton Street side with refrigerators to keep the milk sweet and clean for the babies of local residents.

In the 1930's and 1940's several music programs were held at the Nickerson House including tap dancing, youth little symphony, piano recitals and rhythm bands. It was there that 7-year-old Dacia Libutti, who after being told she was too young to take piano lessons at the House, approached the director to ask to be accepted. The director pointed to the portrait of Lyra and told Dacia "She would have wanted you to learn to play." Dacia started her lessons and has played beautiful music ever since.

The Nickerson House later sponsored outdoor youth camps at bucolic settings in Rhode Island and opened the first supervised playground in the city.[52] In 1945, several children from the Nickerson House were taken for a two-week camping experience at Camp V (for Victory) in Lincoln Woods, Rhode Island. One of these children was 9-year-old Dacia Libutti who today remembers learning to swim there. She became an excellent back-stroker and later used her skills as a lifeguard.

In the 1950's, Brown University instituted a program called Brown Youth Guidance (BYG). Many of their greatest successes came from the tutoring program they conducted through the Nickerson House to the praise of neighborhood schools. It was said that the tutors were as idolized as Ted Williams and Davy Crockett at the time. The expectations of local children were enhanced by BYG athletic programs, scientific and craft projects, and visits to Brown labs and sporting events. BYG arranged for several Nickerson House youth to spend a week in nature at Camp Walt Whitman in New Hampshire. An eight-year-old at Nickerson House commented "I like it when the Brown guys come 'cause they've always got good ideas for us to do."[53]

The Narragansett Brewery donated 59 acres in Coventry, RI in 1958 to the Nickerson House. Named Camp Hamilton, it offered summer activities for city youth including swimming, sports, arts and crafts, dramatics and nature studies.

Among the programs subsequently offered at the Nickerson House were a "charm school" for young women; a Golden Age Center and optometric clinic for senior citizens and a full schedule of adult education courses; for example, high school equivalency, domestic skills, and fitness classes.

When the Nickerson House became the Nickerson Community Center years later, several other humanitarian programs were offered including Head Start, a food pantry, clothing banks and a low-income and homeless veterans housing program called Gateway to Independence. Gateway to Independence was established in 1997 with a $200,000 grant providing 18 beds and an array of services including substance abuse treatment, job referrals and training and mental health services. In 2007, Senator Jack Reed and other officials announced a grant of $600,000 from the Veterans Administration to the Nickerson Community Center for tripling the number of beds available for veterans by providing housing across the street from the Center. Additionally, a handicap accessible van was purchased for homeless veteran transportation.[54]

The Rhode Island YWCA purchased the Nickerson Community Center on the corner of Delaine and Appleton Street in 2015. At the same time, the YWCA also acquired Camp Hamilton in Coventry, RI and the homeless veteran's shelter across Delaine Street., both operated by the Nickerson Community Center. Under the YWCA, the Center leased

---

[53] Bown Alumni Monthly, October 1960.
[54] www.senate.reed.gov.

space to a day care center and opened the Lyra Art Studios for a short time at its primary facility. Until recently, the YWCA continued to provide services to the community through these properties.

A similar neighborhood settlement house that provided health and other programs for Providence's large number of Italian immigrant residents was the Federal Hill House on Atwells Ave.[55] Lyra Brown Nickerson was the hostess of a series of subscription dances held in 1914 at the Churchill House on Angell St. for the benefit of the Federal Hill House.

Belgian Relief

After neutral Belgium was occupied by Germany during the early days of World War I, the Belgian population suffered from a shortage of food and clothing prompting the formation of the Belgian Relief Fund under the direction of future President Herbert Hoover. Lyra's personal "arresting" experiences during the outbreak of hostilities (see next chapter) may have inspired her to hold a subscription dance at the Indoor Tennis Court on December 5th, 1914, to benefit the Belgian Relief Fund. The local Belgian Relief Association effort, under the sponsorship of the Providence Journal, formed a garment committee composed of 14 women including Lyra Brown Nickerson. They collected various kinds of clothing and fabrics for making garments to send to Belgium. The committee issued the following statement: *"We appeal to the people of Rhode Island for a generous response, and will see that all goods are properly shipped to New York, from which point they will be transferred without delay to the destitute men, women and children of Belgium."* Dozens of Providence women were hired to sew and make clothes. Eleven cases of articles were shipped to Europe.[56]

The Irrepressible Society

Five young Providence society ladies from the East Side formed a sewing circle in 1861 which came to be known as the Irrepressible Society. Originally the Society only allowed single women to join and provided work for the needy and instruction in sewing. Their symbol was two pair of scissors crowned by a thimble. The Society was self-supporting by operating a retail store and conducting fund raising events including an annual charity ball and bazaars or rummage sales at local

---

[55] Raben, Jonathan D., *Italian Americans and Federal Hill*, SEVENFISHESPRODUCTION, LLC, 2006.

[56] Providence Daily Journal, *Local Women Organize for Belgian Relief*, Nov. 10, 1914,

churches.[57] The Society provided thousands of layette bundles for the Providence Lying-In (maternity) Hospital. Lyra Brown Nickerson was a member and served as assistant treasurer in 1910. The remnants of the Irrepressible Society morphed into today's Goodwill of Rhode Island.[58]

The Irrepressible Society

Thanks to your kind help, has been able to help many needy cases, and to bring brightness into many homes. We now have forty-one active cases on our books, helping many physically handicapped women to find a place in the community, to feel they are wanted in the world. We have two younger girls, one with no legs, and one with one leg, whom we have taught to use a sewing machine with their artificial limbs. They are now making hospital garments. We turn away between fourteen and fifteen cases a month because we are financially unable to give them employment.

We are a business that is a charity;
  a charity that operates like a business

Tissé spreads, with your monogram $5.00	Blankets bound · · · · $ .25
(require no ironing)	Quilts recovered · · · · 3.00
Runs in stockings mended by expert	Tablecloths and napkins hemmed
Single runs · · · · .25	by hand, per yard · · · .25
Double runs · · · · .35	Butler, maid and kitchen aprons, .75 up

We make anything. See our attractive articles on sale at

THE JUNIOR LEAGUE SHOP

Detail of an advertisement for the Irrepressible Society.[59]

---

[57] https://rhodetour.org/items/show/26.
[58] Boston Globe, Nov. 1910, p.4.
[59] http://tirocchi.stg.brown.edu/514/popups/irrepress_det_popup.html.

3. The Spy

In May of 1914, Lyra Brown Nickerson departed Rhode Island for a three-month tour of Europe. On June 26th of that year, Franz Ferdinand of Austria-Hungary was assassinated by a Serbian in Sarajevo. As fate would have it, Lyra and two friends - Katherine "Kitty" Schermerhorn and Mrs. Conway Evans (the chronicler of the following adventure) arrived in Berlin on July 29, 1914. By that time, Austria-Hungary had declared war on Serbia and Russia, a Serbian ally, mobilized its troops. Germany, an ally of Austria-Hungary, soon declared war on Russia and France, another Russian ally.

The European Adventure

Lyra, Kitty and Mrs. Conway Evans unknowingly had positioned themselves in the midst of the combatants at the dawn of "The Great War."

29. Lyra[60]   30. Kitty[61]   31. Conway Evans[62]

Their motor trip from Berlin to the Holland border by the three women was fraught with danger as they were mistaken for Russian spies. They were told that the frontier was closed and they would have to wait until the war was over. One of their drivers advised them that the actual frontier was at 'Kleine Brucke' and that should be their goal.

The following is an excerpt from Mrs. Conway Evans' account of their "arresting experiences" while attempting to get safe passage home. Her book was dedicated to "MY TWO PLUCKY LITTLE FELLOW PRISONERS."

---

[60] U.S. Passport Applications, Roll 229, 1915 Dec-Jan, Cert. 46116, Image 36.

[61] U.S. Passport Applications, Roll 220, 1915 Jan, Cert. 46700, Image 141.

[62] LA Times, Sept 28 1924.

"Halt." A cordon of soldiers with bayonets across the road put an end to all appreciation of scenery. The "Halt" was very decisive, as well it might be on such an occasion, and we were surrounded by boys— fair-haired, smiling boys, with whom we laughed and talked as much as our limited vocabularies permitted. The chauffeur's pass was produced, and proved satisfactory. If all "Halts" were going to be such friendly affairs, we felt we were in for a merry day. We waived adieus to our youthful soldiers, but within a few hundred yards came another "Halt," and then another, and another. The fifth time we realized hand-waving and friendly salutations were not going to get us very far. Our trunks were to be examined. Our friendly chauffeur pleaded for us, but he was squashed. "This is war time. Examination must be made and no risks taken."[63]

Lyra and her travelling companions were stopped eighteen times before they safely reached the Dutch border. Their dangerous and sometimes embarrassing adventures were chronicled in newspapers across America. The following article included Lyra's own words documenting their travails.

"You see, we three were making a motor car trip through Germany," said Miss Nickerson. "We left Berlin on August 2 in a Gerfan car which we had hired, and the first night got as far as Hanover. There our experience in being 'held up' began...

"It seems that a little before we arrived two Russian spies had actually been arrested. When we got out of our automobile at the hotel, we found ourselves surrounded by an enormous crowd. I could not distinguish what they were shouting at us; except they were demanding that we be questioned.

"A young officer came up through the crowd, saluted, and asked who we were. We showed what papers we had, although there was not a passport among them. The crowd kept shouting that we were Russians, and we kept saying that we were not; that we were Americans, and the officer professed himself satisfied with what credentials we had and we were allowed to enter the hotel.

---

[63] Evans, Conway, *An Account of our Arresting Experiences*, [63] 1914, pp.13-14.

"Everything seemed quiet the next morning, and we got off at 11 o'clock hoping to make the Dutch frontier by that night, our intention being to go on to Rotterdam, where we were sure we could catch the Holland-American steamer. We had had an early breakfast, and as we approached Minden we were looking forward to a good luncheon. We arrived in the town about 2 o'clock and the first thing we saw was four soldiers standing in the middle of the street with their guns at their shoulders. You may imagine that we halted very promptly.

AMERICAN WOMEN SEARCHED AS SPIES

MISTAKEN FOR RUSSIANS, PARTY OF YOUNG WOMEN ARE SUBJECTED TO RIGOROUS EXAMINATION AND NARROWLY ESCAPE LYNCHING.

"The soldiers took down our baggage and opened every trunk and bag we had. When they had finished, they took us to the headquarters of the military commander of that district, where we were asked a lot of questions. Then we were led into a room and kept there for half an hour, with a soldier on guard. At the end of that time the commander handed us a passport, a piece of white paper, which said that the three ladies had been examined that They were not spies, and that They had nothing of a suspicious nature with them. That passport was of great assistance, and helped us through at almost every one of the eighteen points that we were stopped that day.

"At a little place called Rheine however, it proved ineffectual. There we ran plumb into a mob of almost 500 people, in front of which were two soldiers with guns. They made Mrs. Evans get out of the automobile and walk to the office of the commander where she had to show our passports and swear in her best German that we were what we claimed to be. While we were waiting for her to return, the mob pressed about us and became abusive. Several of them struck me on the head with their fists but I was more scared than hurt. However, we were not kept long, and when Mrs. Evans came back and climbed into the car the soldiers waved their hands and shouted to the crowd and it parted and let us through.

"But when we got to Groneau, which is about a quarter of an hour from the Dutch frontier, we found fifteen soldiers drawn up across the road, each with his rifle up, pointing it at us. Of course, we stopped at once.

"The discovery of nothing suspicious in the car or our baggage did not satisfy them. They marched us off to an inn and took us upstairs and cross-examined each of us. Then they had us sign our names and they inspected our signatures carefully. Then they sent each of us to a separate room each of us in charge of two women. These undressed us until we had not a shred of clothes on. Mrs. Evans' two female guards even went so far as to take down her hair, in the apparent belief that it contained dispatches.

"This being done, they permitted us to dress again. Before we were led away to be stripped the officers apologized profusely, and after the search was finished, they repeated their apologies, saying that they had done this only because they had to follow orders. Well, they did not allow us to go to bed until a quarter of 2 o'clock in the morning, and all night there was a patrol of soldiers and police dogs outside our window.

"The next morning, they made another examination of our luggage, and when we lunched, one of the women who had searched us sat at table with us.

"After luncheon we were permitted to get into our car and a patrol escorted us to the border.

When the three women reached the border of Holland, they found that "Kleine Brucke" (meaning "little bridge") was too small for a motor car crossing and they would have to cross by foot. They were able to walk across and acquired transportation to Amsterdam.

The route out of the German Empire territory is shown below: Over 400 miles over rough roads using very slow automobiles.

The three intrepid itinerants were able to reach Amsterdam where they encountered George Stephenson from South Bend, Indiana., George, his mother and cousin were also seeking to return home. Lyra told him about how rudely she had been searched by German women and that her gold handbag was snatched away from her by a pompous German soldier because he thought it was a bomb. It was later returned but he had Lyra open it herself in case it was explosive. The Stephansons had their own problems getting to Amsterdam. They were able get the last train out of Berlin as nearby German citizens sang "Die Wacht am Rhein"[64] (Watch on the Rhine) but had to change trains three times and had their baggage opened and searched on the tracks. The Stephensons narrowly escaped a German mob in at a cafe in Munich rioting because they were not allowed to sing "Die Wacht am Rhein."

One of Lyra's party chartered an automobile to the port at Rotterdam to secure passage to America. On the day before the *Nieuw Amsterdam* was scheduled to sail, George stood in line from 5 AM to 3:30 PM and was able to get six tickets in the ship's engineer cabins for Lyra's and his own parties. A total of about 1200 fleeing Americans were crammed into the steamer and many wealthy passengers had to travel in steerage or the baggage hold because of their difficulty in obtaining money in Europe.

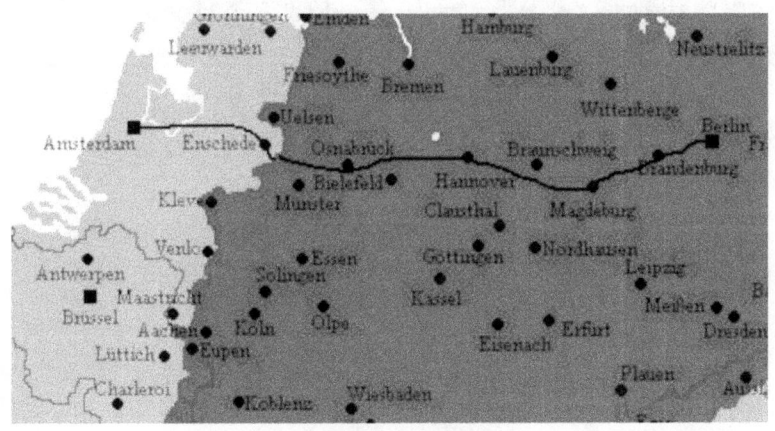

32. The Escape Route

The voyage across the Atlantic proved to be an extremely dangerous journey. The *Nieuw Amsterdam* was challenged three times by torpedo boats. Initially, she was stopped by a Dutch torpedo destroyer. Later, four British torpedo cruisers came along side. The flagship fired two warning shots and sped towards the *Nieuw Amsterdam*. After some cordial communications, the *Amsterdam* was allowed to proceed. The final encounter came when about 400 miles from Nova Scotia. The cruiser *H.M.S. Essex* chased but could not overtake, so she fired two warning shots for the *Nieuw Amsterdam* to slow down and identify itself.

---

[64]"Die Wacht am Rhein" was sung by the German soldiers at Rick's Café in *Casablanca*.

Satisfied of the ship's neutrality, the Essex allowed Lyra's ship to go on to the safety of New York Harbor.

33. Challenged by Flagship

---

[65] The Montclair Times (N.J.), 26 Aug 1914, T. Louis Hansen.

Who was Conway Evans?

More should be said about the chronicler of this "adventure." Mrs. Conway Evans was a very noteworthy woman in her own right.

She was born Louisa Conway Pitman in 1877 in British Guiana to sugar plantation owner Augustus Pitman. After the Pitmans returned to live in England, she was wed in what was described as a fashionable wedding to Welch Major Edward Walter David Evans in 1904.[66] Miss Pitman thus became Mrs. Conway Evans. The marriage in Devon, England was a local attraction primarily because of the reputations of the couple, especially Miss Pitman. Augustus held the distinction of being a Master of Otter Hounds. Hounding otters was later outlawed in Britain. Major Evans went on to become the Sheriff of Cardigan.

Mrs. Evans had travelled extensively before the "adventure" and was in great demand for her entertaining lectures about the many lands she had visited. At the time of her European spy story, she lived in Florence, Italy and later in California and England.

Conway became heavily involved in social issues such as woman's suffrage, industrial labor conditions, and politics. In 1921, addressing the National Unionist Association, she advocated woman's use of the vote to ameliorate working conditions.[67] Later in the 1930's, Mrs. Conway Evans gave a series of lectures relating the lives of prominent women - many with whom she had personal contact.[68]

In a 1939 lecture about the historic background of the Thames River, Mrs. Evans told the story of an American who said the Thames was "not a river, but a crick." MP John Burns replied "You are not looking at a river, but Living History!"[69]

Mrs. Conway Evans continued her travelogue lectures across the U.S., Canada and Europe about her South American heritage and European locales at so-called "Magic Lantern" lectures using the precursor of the slide projector to add visuals to her presentations. In one of her lectures about her birthplace, she took the opportunity to lavishly praise Prime Minister Stanley Baldwin of the Conservative Party.

---

[66] Western Times, Devon, England June 29, 1904.

[67] Somerset Standard, Somerset, England, 2 Sept. 1921.

[68] Middlesex Advertiser and Country Gazette, Mar 1936.

[69] Times Colonist, 25 Oct. 1939.

Because of Conway's encyclopedic knowledge of travel destinations, Lyra Brown Nickerson engaged Mrs. Conway Evans to be her guide and chaperone in travels to South America as well as Europe. The three "plucky prisoners" Lyra, Kitty and Mrs. Evans in January 1915 went on a four-month tour of South America on the SS Kroonland, one of the world's largest passenger ships at the time.

34. SS Kroonland in the Panama Canal -February 1915[70]

..

---

[70] ggarchive.com/Ocean Travel/Immigration ships/Kroonland.

4. The Aviatrix

Lyra enthusiastically embraced the latest technology. While spending the summer with her parents at the Hesperus House in the Magnolia section of Gloucester, MA in 1905, Lyra was described as the "most enthusiastic motorist on the shore" who drove a party of her friends to Newburyport.[71] In 1911, she registered a 17 horsepower "runabout" motorcar, the Hupmobile. Later in 1915, she registered her next roadster, a Scripps-Booth classic.

35. Hupmobile   *36. Scripps-Booth*

Six years after their first flight at Kitty Hawk in 1903, the Wright Brothers supplied the first military airplane to the U.S. Army signal Corps in response to government specifications. The Wright Military Flyer piloted by Orville passed all requirements after a previous attempt in 1908 by the Wrights had ended with a crash, killing the military passenger and seriously injuring Orville. The Wright plane was the only aircraft in service by the military for the next two years, but by 1914, both the Army and Navy operated aviation squads.[72]

By 1915, aviation, particularly military aviation, was still only in its infancy. The number of commissioned military airplanes was estimated to be only a few dozen at the time. The idea of taking flight intrigued Lyra. She had taken to the air in Germany over Berlin in a Zeppelin, and had a burning desire to be involved with "aeroplanes."

On returning from Germany, Lyra was said to be passenger on a monoplane for daily flights over Providence. On one her many stops in Rhode Island, legendary aviatrix and stunt pilot Ruth Law took Lyra on a flight as a passenger. When Ruth offered oil baron John D. Rockefeller such a ride, he replied "I'll wait till my wings grow."

---

[71] *North Shore Breeze, Vol.2*,1905, p. 18.
[72] www.si.edu/object/1909 wright-mobility flyer.

Her interest in aviation prompted Lyra to contribute $500 to the Aero Club of America fund and later $7500 to purchase a Sturtevant seaplane for the Aviation Division of the Rhode Island National Guard. In addition, Lyra contributed a tender boat to launch, fuel and resupply the seaplane. Lyra's contribution was the second largest contribution to the fund, the largest being $40,762 and seven aeroplanes by Mrs. Thomas A. Edison, Chairman of the Naval Advisory Board of Inventions.

When told of the $7500 average cost of an aeroplane, Lyra replied *"I feel that our essential need at present is aeroplanes, and I shall be too glad to help with the good work the Aero Club of America is doing to supply the Militia with machines and train officers of the Militia to fly. As the Militia is the backbone of our defenses, it ought to have aeroplanes."*

37. Sturtevant Seaplane

The Sturtevant Model S3 seaplane being used for instructive purposes by the Rhode Island Naval Militia It is powered by a 140 H.P. eight-cylinder Sturtevant motor.

The boys in Aviation Corps took such a liking to Lyra that they dubbed her the "Little Major" and named her donated hydro-aeroplane "Lyra." Many years before Amelia Earhart became a household name for her flights, Lyra was flying over Narragansett Bay from Quonset Point to Newport and return with Sturtevant instructor Roderick W. Wright.

38. Lyra Ready for Takeoff

39. Lyra and R.W. Wright Over Narragansett Bay[73]

After her flight, Lyra wrote to the Providence Journal: *"I had the pleasure of making a flight last Wednesday in Rhode Island's new seaplane, which weighs 2150 pounds and is 45 feet and 8 inches spread. She has an eight-cylinder, 140 horse-power motor, and has a speed of 80 miles an hour, her fuselage is of steel."*[74]

---

[73] Photographs by Raymond N. Estey.
[74] Providence Sunday Journal, *For the State's Aerial Service*, Lyra Brown Nickerson, July 1916.

Lyra's submission to the Journal was an appeal to the Rhode Island Legislature to provide monies for properly equipping, paying and training the Aviation Corps of the state militia. She cited several needs such as rubber boots for the "28 picked men" of the Corps as they were "wading out in their ordinary clothes."

Lyra's flight was documented by Raymond N. Estey, aerial photographer for the Westerly American and Providence newspapers. He was also a member of the Aviation Corps of the Rhode Island National Guard and his thoughts about the value of air power echoed those of Lyra. The U.S. had deployed troops to the Mexican border at El Paso in 1916 responding to the raids by revolutionary Mexican leader Pancho Villa. Estey advocated stationing 1000 aircraft on the border to give us a distinct advantage over a country that had no air defense.[75]

40. Raymond Estey and "Lyra"

Raymond continued to be an advocate for air power. He was particularly concerned about the lack of trained American pilots.[76] He also feared that Japan could launch a surprise aerial attack. He speculated that the target could be the Panama Canal to cripple our shipping and prevent access to the Pacific. Estey was scheduled to join the LaFayette Escadrille American volunteer fliers but the group was disbanded before he could serve. When America entered the war, Raymond enlisted and saw service as an "Eye in the Sky" surveillance photographer. Raymond Estey was inducted into the Rhode Island Aviation Hall of Fame in 2018.

---

[75] Bridgeport Times and Evening Farmer, June 29, 1916.
[76] Hartford Courant, Mar 25, 1917, *Aviator Estey on Our Present Predicament.*

Lyra's gift prompted many others across the nation to contribute to the Aero Club of America, fostering a build-up of the nation's aviation capability prior to our entry into World War I. The Rhode Island subscription list was started by the donation from Lyra. Rhode Island Governor Beechman followed with a $500 donation to the fund. The smallest state soon had a total contribution of over $18,000, which formed the funding nucleus for an aviation corps. Subsequently, the U.S. government offered to train militia aviation officers and President Wilson instituted a program to form three aviation squadrons at a cost of $7,500,000.[77]

Lyra loved being airborne, planned to purchase her own craft and dreamed of being a part of Uncle Sam's air corps as an aviatrix. When the U.S. entered WW1, aviatrix Ruth Law was the first woman to enlist in the Army and volunteered to join the aviation corps but was refused because of her sex. Instead, she formed a "Flying Circus" of pilots and barnstormed across the country.

Lyra's exploits in the wild blue yonder were reported as widely in the press all over the country as were her social activities.

41. Aviatrix

---

[77] Washington Herald, *Eighteen National Guard Flying Corps Organized to Aid national Defense*, Nov.21, 1915, p.30,

42. At Quonset

    Perhaps inspired by Lyra and other female aviation pioneers, another College Hill heiress, Mary Ann Lippitt joined the Postal Service as an aviator during World War II. Mary Ann was the daughter of textile millionaire and U.S. Senator Henry F. Lippitt, half-sister of Lyra's contemporary Louise Lippitt and sister of philanthropist and prominent Rhode Island political figure Freddy Lippitt. Like Raymond Estey, Mary Ann is enshrined in the RI Aviation Hall of Fame.

"If you want your teeth to rattle and if you want to be thrilled to the marrow, you should go up in a flying machine." -Lyra Brown Nickerson

5. The Betrothed

Lyra Nickerson surprisingly became engaged to Henry Garfield Clark in the late summer of 1916. The anticipation of their marriage prompted great celebration by the holding of many festive dinners. The Boston Post wrote a feature article about the soon-to-be wife Lyra and husband Henry. Here is the article in its entirety:

Boston Sunday Post August 6, 1916
"LOVE, LUCK AND AEROPLANES IN ROMANCE OF ATHLETIC DIRECTOR AND $6,000,000 HEIRESS"

Love, luck and aeroplanes!
Six million dollars, patience, pluck and perseverance!
These are the factors in the latest romance of the social set at Narragansett Pier.
In the announcement of the engagement of Miss Lyra Brown Nickerson, the popular Providence heiress and aviatress, to Henry G. Clark, assistant athletic director of Brown University, last week a romance was uncovered which many of the intimate friends of the happy couple did not even suspect.
Decadent members of European mobility have no charms for Miss Nickerson. An athletic, all-American girl herself, Miss Nickerson has chosen as a husband a man who is a typical young American man who proved his worth by faithful observance of the old motto, "If at first you don't succeed, try, try again."

A Democratic Heiress

Six-million-dollar heiresses don't grow on every bush, and it was a surprise to the reporter to find Miss Nickerson as democratic as she is charming.
"I suppose you want to know all about my past." she smiled "But really, there isn't much to tell."
"I have known Mr. Clark for over 11 years and he has been wooing me for a long time. It was not until a short time ago that I definitely made up my mind to accept him, however."
"What was it that decided you?" the reporter asked.

Miss Nickerson flushed becomingly. "I think it was his perseverance." she said laughingly. "We had been close friends for a good many years and, of course, I knew he wanted to marry me. But somehow, I couldn't quite make up my mind and settle down."

"You know I am fond of all kinds of outdoor sport, and so is Mr. Clark. Consequently, I have been so busy enjoying myself that I have hesitated to assume the responsibilities of marriage.

"However, Mr. Clark proved so faithful and took everything so good-naturally, that I finally decide to say 'Yes' and now we are to be married on the 4th of October." she concluded with a smile.

"About those aeroplane flights of yours----" the reporter began.

Enjoyed Aerial Trip

"Oh, yes." she interrupts. "But you mean hydroplanes. I was down to Quonset last week and went up 2500 feet in the Rhode Island plane and enjoyed the trip immensely."

"Weren't you afraid?"

"Not the last time. This wasn't my first trip, you know. An aeroplane is a great thing to take pictures from, and, after one gets used to it, it's great sport to go photographing with the birds.

"But now I've to get dressed. I'm going to Providence tonight and must ask you to excuse me for the present. I don't want to run away from you, but you know how it is."

With this Miss Nickerson departed, leaving behind her recollections of happy smiles, chestnut hair and dark brown eyes that gleamed with mischief and the health that goes with outdoor life.

Miss Nickerson stands 5 feet 4 inches, and is of slender build, but evidently very wiry and active. She loves golf, tennis, and all other forms of out-door sport. Her photographs do not do her justice and her looks are surpassed only by her charm of manner. All of whom she comes in contact are attracted to her and the reporter heard many favorable comments on her kindly heart and helpful charities.

Her chauffeur shed considerable light on the secret of her popularity when he said:

"When it comes to work for anybody, they don't make 'em any better than Miss Nickerson. I have been driving her for eight years now and I hope to still be on the job when I'm 80.

"In all the time I've been in her employ I've never heard her speak a cross word or known her to do an unkind act."

"As to her fiancé, the chauffeur said he was "a real man and a thorough gentleman."

A later interview with Mr. Clark certainly corroborated this opinion.

When speaking of her aeroplane flights, Miss Nickerson did not inform the reporter that she contributed $7500 out of her own pocket to help the State of Rhode Island purchase the new Sturtevant seaplane that was recently acquired.

Neither did she say that two years ago she spent $18,000 to erect a large, glass-enclosed tennis court at East Providence, where, since its completion, many well-known tennis players have been entertained and taken part in tournaments.

Nor did she hint that she had the reputation of being one of the most big-hearted and philanthropic women of Providence.

And she did not state that her giving had not been of the abstract kind that more than one wealthy personage has indulged in, but that she had endeavored to be of real assistance to many of those in need and had never refused an appeal for aid in any worthy cause.

Miss Nickerson is the daughter of the late Mr. and Mrs. Edward I. Nickerson of Providence R.I. and the granddaughter of Joseph Brown, one of the founders of the Brown & Sharpe Manufacturing Company.

Much of the income from the immense fortune left her by her parents and grandparents is devoted to charity, and is largely through her efforts and contributions that the aviation corps of the Rhode Island National Guard was made possible. Her latest donation to the corps is a gasoline tender, which is used in launching and caring for the big Sturdivant hydroplane.

Note: The following headline appeared in the Minneapolis Morning Star. Lyra truly led the "strenuous" life advocated by President Teddy Roosevelt. Henry Clark was called a "model man" because he did not smoke, drink or swear.

Strenuous Girl Heiress Will Marry a Model Young Man

He Personifies "Perseverance"

After talking to Mr. Clark, one's first impression of him is that he is a sturdy, up-standing man who knows what he wants and goes out and gets it.

A single glance at his sun-tanned face and firm, well-moulded chin made it instantly clear why Miss Nickerson said that it was his "perseverance" that won her. His features indicate unusual strength of character and an indomitable will that refuses to recognize any obstacles.

43. Henry Clark

He stands about five feet seven inches and weighs approximately 168 pounds. His shoulders are carried well back and he looks the whole world in the face when he talks, while his smile seems like a ray of sunshine.

Mr. Clark comes from old Rhode Island stock and was born in Shannock, R.I., the son of George H. and Lillian (Carr) Clark. He is a descendant of the Oliver Hazard Perry family.

His father is one of the managing officials of the Columbia Fabric Company of Shannock, and he also has a brother, George Perry Clark who is another official of this company. One of his sisters, Miss Harriet B. Clark, is a graduate of Smith College, while the other sister, Florence, graduated from Wellesley, afterward taking a course at Columbia Art School.

Mr. Clark was graduated from Brown in 1907 and is a member of Delta Phi Fraternity, the University and other Providence clubs. He is very fond of swimming, tennis, football and baseball and took a prominent part in athletics while at Brown.

After his academic education was finished, Mr. Clark was engaged as an instructor in the Friends School in Providence, and went from there to Brown as assistant athletic director. He stayed in this position for about two years and then resigned to accept a position in his father's mills at Shannock, but his love of athletics proved too strong and in a short time he returned to his old occupation at Brown, where he has since been employed.

His manner is quiet and unassuming, and is only when his fiancé is being spoken of that he lets go of his feelings.

"She is a wonderful girl." He exclaimed enthusiastically, adding a moment later, "And I'm a very lucky man!"

"I have known her for years and first met her through one of her cousins during my student days at Brown.

"I don't know how long I've loved her. Ever since we first met, I guess, but it was a long time before I dared to hope that the day might come when I would wed her.

"Our marriage ought to be a very successful one, for our likes and dislikes are similar, and I am sure we are going to be very happy."

The article ended with that optimistic quote from Henry. Sadly, his outlook was not to be the case.

6. The Tragedy

Lyra and Henry's upcoming nuptials on October 4 were celebrated by a multitude of parties and balls in Providence and Narragansett. The social agenda had to be exhausting for the bride-to-be and tragically ended with Lyra becoming gravely ill.
The following memory was published in early August.

A Pleasant Remembrance.

"I must express my pleasure of the recent story on the social page of The News concerning the approaching marriage of Miss Lyra Nickerson, of Providence, R. I.," said Miss Laura Templeton. "I remember Miss Nickerson quite well, having met her at the Black and White Ball in this city last Spring. She wore a Pierrot costume, the same one in which she led a similar function at Providence and at which she realized two thousand dollars for charity. Bright, versatile and interesting, Miss Nickerson charmed all who were so fortunate as to meet her here."

Initially, the belief was that Lyra was suffering from ptomaine food poisoning and would recover for her wedding.[78] The heading in the Washington Herald read "RICH SOCIETY GIRL VICTIM OF PTOMAINE" and reported *"She is widely known as a tennis player, swimmer and driver of automobiles."*

Dr. Charles Hitchcock, New York physician and seasonal resident of Narragansett Pier, attended to Lyra. Dr. Hitchcock was born and lived his early life in Providence with his parents Charles Sr. and Olivia (Cowell) as well as his siblings, George and "Minnie" (Amelia). His father and brother were both artists of note. Charles Sr. was a distinguished portrait painter and George was recognized as an impressionist master during his lifetime.

---

[78] *The Washington Herald,* Washington, D.C., "Rich Girl Victim of Ptomaine", Aug. 30, 1916, p.6.

> MISS LYRA B. NICKERSON OF THIS
> CITY DEAD AT NARRAGANSETT PIER
>
> Popular Young Society Woman Victim of Enteric Fever After a Two Weeks Illness.

44. Notice of Passing[79]

The truth was that Lyra had contracted typhoid fever (called enteric fever in some newspapers) and would succumb to the disease. Dr. Hitchcock believed she had come down with the disease on her recent two-week automobile trip around New England. Her death on August 30, 1916 was reported across the country with headlines;[80] for example, the following that appeared in the *Richmond (Indiana) Item*:

PROSPECTIVE BRIDE DIES AS RESULT OF TOO MANY PARTIES

---

[79] Providence Journal, August 31, 1916.
[80] Newspapers.com.

The Washington Evening Star: **RICH BRIDE-ELECT DIES, A VICTIM OF FESTIVITIES-Friends of Miss Lyra Brown Nickerson Arranged Too Many Engagement Entertainments**
The Boston Post: **DIES ON EVE OF WEDDING-Rhode Island's Wealthiest Girl Typhoid Victim**
The Salt Lake City Herald-Republican: **HEIRESS DIES ON EVE OF WEDDING-Miss Lyra Brown Nickerson, Worth $6,000,000, was to Marry "Model Man"**
The New Britain Herald: **STRENUOUS LIFE FATAL-Wealthy Young Woman Feted by Friends After Engagement, Unable to Stand Ravages of Illness**

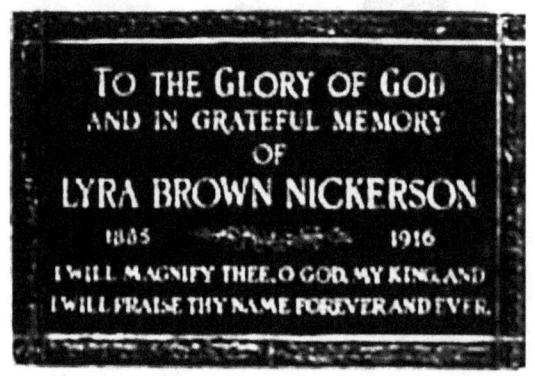

45. Memorial Plaque

Earlier in the year, Lyra had donated a $5000 organ to the Trinity Episcopal Church in Pawtucket, Rhode Island. In grateful memory of her and to the glory of God, Trinity placed the above bronze tablet in the church. Members of the church and children of the Sunday School had provided for the cost of the Gorham Company tablet. It was veiled in a screen of pink rosebuds for the initial presentation which was removed after an address by the rector.

The tennis committee of the Agawam Hunt Club put off for one year all the tournaments of the ladies championship matches for Rhode Island because of Lyra's sudden death. Lyra had been a member of the committee and donor of the championship challenge cup.[81]

---

[81] Boston Globe, 8 Sept 1916, p. 7.

This photo below of the "Little Major" was published in the September 11, 1916 edition of Aerial Age showing her standing in front of the Sturtevant seaplane "Lyra.".[82]

46. With the "Boys"

Miss Lyra Brown Nickerson of Providence, who died on August 30th, is standing with the officers of the Aviation Corps, Rhode Island Naval Battalion in front of the Sturtevant seaplane which she presented to the organization only a few weeks before her death. Miss Nickerson was enthusiastically devoted to aviation, and the loss of her generous support to the art will be keenly felt.

---

[82] Aerial Age, Vol. 3, Sept. 11, 1916, p.775.

After a private funeral at her home on Angell Street, Lyra was laid to rest at Swan Point Cemetery in Providence next to her parents, and grandfather Joseph Rogers Brown with his wives.[83]

47. Swan Point Gravestone

---

[83] Findagrave.com, Swan Point Cemetery, Group 17, Lot1, Space 3.

7. The Legacy

In her will, witnessed and presumably prepared by Richard B. Comstock, Lyra remembered several of the significant people in her short life; but the bulk of her fortune would be left as a legacy to two Rhode Island institutions.

Special Bequests

Several special people in her life were given specific bequests totaling $260,000 in Lyra's will, including her travelling companion Mrs. Conway Evans ($5000), Harriet Talbot ($5000), cousins Bertha and Eleanor Nickerson ($5000 each), cousins Edward and Ralph Williams ($5000 each), five members of the Plummer family ($5000 each), her housemate and cousin Jane Brown Jones ($50,000), and her Irish servants-Alice Curry, Ellen Curry and Margaret Johnston ($10,000 each) for *"faithful service of said legatees to my mother and since her death, to me."* Lyra remembered her lifelong friend, Beatrice Brown Berry, by leaving her home at 71 Angell Street to her. The Berrys continued to live there through the war years until they moved to New York City. The 63 Angell St. property owned by Lyra adjacent to her home was designated to be given to Vinton Medbury, an assistant at Edward I. Nickerson's architectural firm. Vinton had died in 1915 so the house was passed on to Vinton's son, Royal. Lyra willed to another classmate, Lucy Cameron Sammis, the property at 57 University Avenue. One Mary Elizabeth Pendleton of Missouri was given $10,000 and a $12,600 trust fund was established for the benefit of Mrs. Patrick McCaughey and her children.[84]

---

[84] Providence Daily Journal, *Public Bequests in Nickerson Will,* Sept. 7, 1916.

Henry Garfield Clark

Her betrothed, Henry Clark, was unfortunately not included in her will. Dr. Hitchcock noted that Lyra was too ill to make any changes on her deathbed; however, Henry was independently wealthy. He was a vice president of the Clark family textile business, the Columbia Narrow Fabric Company in the village of Shannock, RI. While still the athletic director at Brown in 1921, he married Mildred H. Maynard Dickinson and according the 1925 census; they lived on College St. in Providence. Henry later married Marjorie Peugnet in 1934. Like Lyra, Marjorie was another society dame. Marjorie was a well-known mezzo contralto concert singer and came from an affluent family in Yonkers, NY. Her father was a vice president of the Silk Association which later became the Federal Textiles Industries Association. Her mother had Rhode Island roots, descended from Rowland Robinson, an early settler of Narragansett. The Peugnet family summered in Rhode Island.

48. Henry and Marjorie

The Clarks hosted a tour of their Home "Shanamar" at the 55th reunion of the Brown University Class of 1907 as they had done on many previous occasions. Henry and E. Tudor Gross served as officers together in the Brown Alumni Association for many years. Henry and Marjorie lived in Shannock until the end of their lives in 1978. They are buried in the Clark Family Cemetery. Another tragedy befell Henry on September 21, 1938. His mother Celia and two of his sisters were drowned at Charlestown Beach in Rhode Island from the storm surge associated with the unnamed and unexpected hurricane of that year.

Alice Lahey Foster

Her dear friend from school days, Alice Lahey Foster, was to be her matron of honor at her wedding to Henry Clark. Alice thought so well of Lyra that she named her daughter Lyra Nickerson Foster.[85] Lyra's will designates Alice and little Lyra as beneficiaries as written in the Alabama papers: [86]

49. Lyra Nickerson Foster

Birmingham Woman Gets $25,000; Little Girl, $5,000

---

[85] Findagrave.com, photo, Lyra Nickerson Foster Smith, Oakwood Cemetery, Montgomery, AL.
[86] Huntsville Times (AL), 11 Sep 1916.

Providence Public Library and RISD

After several bequests by Lyra to organizations including the Grace Episcopal Church, Rhode Island Hospital, the Providence Day Nursery Association, the Irrepressible Society, and the Society for the Prevention of Cruelty to Children; there remained about $3,000,000 to be divided equally between the Providence Public Library and the Rhode Island School of Design (RISD) in agreement with the wishes of her mother's will.

The $1.5 million given to the Library filled a dire need for funding and made the present Rhode Island system of libraries possible. It was the largest single bequest to an American library in 1916. The cost of maintenance of the library and its four branches rose so greatly that it could only be met by tripling the city's appropriation. When the City of Providence temporarily diminished the appropriation, the library was saved by Lyra's bequest which had by then yielded $2,500,000.[87] Any person now leaving money to the Library becomes a member of the Lyra Brown Nickerson Society.

The Rhode Island School of Design used their $1.5 million along with the addition of many works of art contributed by Lyra to found the RISD Museum of Art. The fine art had been collected by her father during his international travels with his wife, which had included a 4-year "Grand Tour" of Europe prior to Lyra's birth.[88]

In support of the jewelry manufacturing industry in Rhode Island, Lyra's bequest was also used to construct a Jewelry and Silversmithing Building for RISD in 1921.[89] At the dedication, RISD President Mrs. Gustave Radeke spoke as follows: "For the fund which made it possible, the Rhode Island School of Design is indebted to the noble bequest of Miss Lyra Brown Nickerson." and Providence Mayor Joseph Grainer said "The community is deeply indebted ...especially to the late Lyra Brown Nickerson." The top three industries in Rhode Island at that time were tools and machinery, exemplified by Brown and Sharpe, woolen textiles and jewelry. Rhode Island was called the "jewelry capital of the world." RISD's training of artisans helped maintain Rhode Island as a leader in the industry throughout the 20th century.

---

[87] Library Journal, Feb. 1, 1927, vol 52, iss 3, *The Providence Public Library Looks Ahead.*

[88] Wikipedia entry for Edward I. Nickerson.

[89] https://digitalcommons.risd.edu/, *Bulletin of the Rhode Island School of Design,* Vol, IX, Apr. 1921, p.14,

The chairman of the Advisory Committee for the new building was Harold Ostby, brother of Lyra's friend and Titanic survivor Helen Ostby. A jewelry museum and library were established at RISD in memory of their father, Englehart Ostby, who had perished in the Titanic disaster.

50. Jewelry Bench Room

From the October 1916 edition of the Bulletin of the Rhode Island School of 'Design:

In the death of Miss Lyra Brown Nickerson, the Rhode Island School of Design has lost a member and friend who had shown for years in numberless ways her deep interest in its work. Her father, Mr. Edward I. Nickerson, was for twenty-four years a Trustee of the School of Design and served for many years with much ability and fidelity upon the Executive Committee. Visitors to the Museum have often had the privilege of enjoying the fine works of art collected by him in Italy and in Egypt. It will be the duty of the Rhode Island School of Design to use the noble bequest left by Miss Nickerson in ways that will keep in beautiful and enduring memory the name of one who showed herself in her short life to be one of the most generous and public-spirited citizens of our State.[90]

---

[90] https://digitalcommons.risd.edu/, *Bulletin of the Rhode Island School of Design*, Vol IV, Oct. 1916, p.2.

Epilogue/Conclusion

Lyra Brown Nickerson's impact on Providence and Rhode Island is immeasurable. Her largesse is still felt today by all whose lives were enriched by the Nickerson House on Delaine Street, the Providence Library System and the Rhode Island School of Design as well as by many other unseen beneficiaries. Lyra was a pioneer in the establishment of aviation as a force in national defense, the introduction of indoor tennis to Rhode Island, and most importantly for young Dacia Libutti who became my wife, and countless other Rhode Islanders, the establishment of the Nickerson House in Providence. Biographer William Richard Cutter expressed it well when he paraphrased lines from Wordsworth's *She Was a Phantom of Delight*:

"A Perfect Woman, nobly planned
To guide, to comfort, and command"

51. Perfect Woman

---

[91] Fuoco, Joe; *Rhode Island Mill Villages*; Image courtesy of Nickerson Community Center.

She Was a Phantom of Delight

BY WILLIAM WORDSWORTH
She was a Phantom of delight
When first she gleamed upon my sight;
A lovely Apparition, sent
To be a moment's ornament;
Her eyes as stars of Twilight fair;
Like Twilight's, too, her dusky hair;
But all things else about her drawn
From May-time and the cheerful Dawn;
A dancing Shape, an Image gay,
To haunt, to startle, and way-lay.
I saw her upon nearer view,
A Spirit, yet a Woman too!
Her household motions light and free,
And steps of virgin-liberty;
A countenance in which did meet
Sweet records, promises as sweet;
A Creature not too bright or good
For human nature's daily food;
For transient sorrows, simple wiles,
Praise, blame, love, kisses, tears, and smiles.
And now I see with eye serene
The very pulse of the machine;
A Being breathing thoughtful breath,
A Traveller between life and death;
The reason firm, the temperate will,
Endurance, foresight, strength, and skill;
A perfect Woman, nobly planned,
To warn, to comfort, and command;
And yet a Spirit still, and bright
With something of angelic light.

Appendix A: Family Ties
Relationship of author to Lyra Brown Nickerson

**Nickerson Progenitor (7th cousin once removed)
From Nickerson Family Association records**

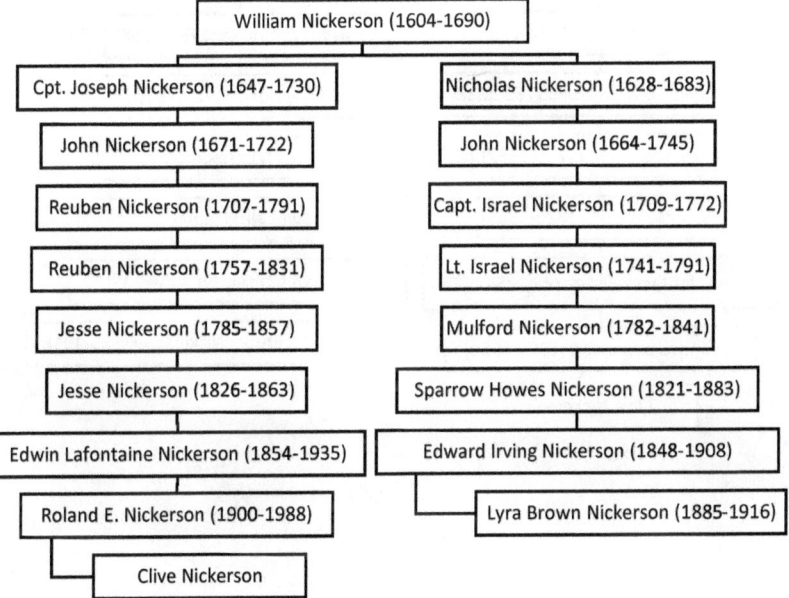

Sparrow Progenitor (6th cousin once removed)
From familysearch.com records

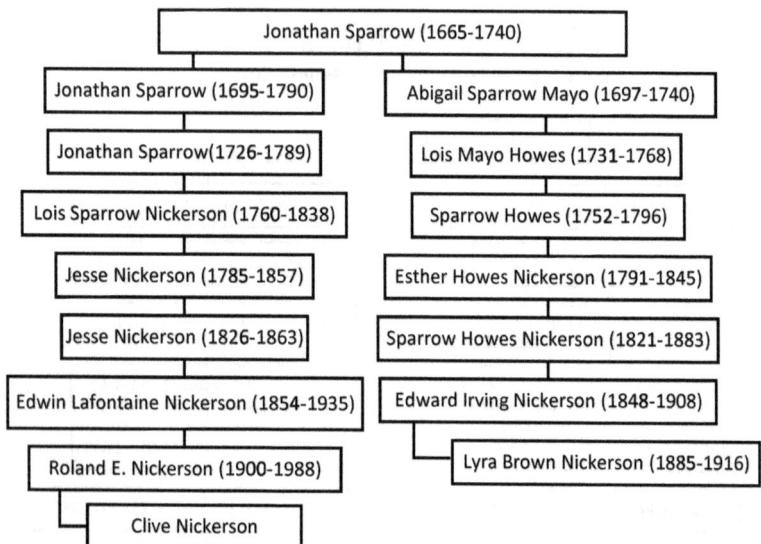

Appendix B: Nickerson Designed Houses

Several historic Providence homes were designed by Edward Irving Nickerson, Lyra Brown Nickerson's father. Edward was known for his Queen Anne style structures which were described at the time as "Nickersonian." Listed below are some of the most notable houses on the East Side of Providence with descriptions taken from the *Guide to Providence Architecture* by William McKensie Woodward.[92]

52. Arnold House[93]

Newton Arnold House (1988), 24 Stimson Ave. Queen Anne design, Used as a backdrop for the movie "Ragtime," Set designer Eugene Lee was a nearby resident.

Dr. George Weaton Carr House (1885), 29 Waterman St., across from the First Baptist Church. Edward I. Nickerson applied architectural methods

---

[92] Providence Preservation Society, *Guide to Providence Architecture,* William McKensie Woodward, E. A. Johnson, 2003.
[93] Newton D. Arnold House, 1888, 24 Stimson Avenue, Providence, Rhode Island (victorianweb.org), Photograph by George P. Landow.

from his extensive library which was donated by Lyra Brown Nickerson to the Providence Public Library after her father's death.

Jesse Colman House (1894), 272 President Ave., A modest wood frame house.

Stephen Cooke House, (1889), 158 Bowen St., Extensive ornamentation by "The most flamboyant of Providence's late 19th century architects."

Seril Dodge House II, (Providence Art Club 1886), 11 Thomas St. Interior reworked by Edward I. Nickerson, Art Club member.

Joseph Hartshorn House (1883) and Mary Hartwell House (1884), 81 and 77 Parade St., Joseph and Mary were fraternal twins, complementary designs, Nickerson at the top of his game, described as "drop-dead gorgeous."

Byron and Helen Potter House, (1894-1899), 8 Stimson Ave. Simplification in a form stylish in the 90's v. earlier Queen Anne elaborate designs, evokes Frank Lloyd Wright.

Charles Sprague House (1894), 44 Stimson Ave. Similar to Potter design, departure from Queen Anne detailing.

George Wilkinson House (1890), 153 Ontario Ave., Queen Anne and Neo-Tudor composite.

Bibliography

Aerial Age, v.3, September 11,1916, p.775.

Anthony, O. Dale, private email, Aug. 7, 2017, information concerning Edward I. Nickerson, Lyra Frances Brown and Lyra Brown Nickerson.

Boston Sunday Post, Aug 6, 1916, "*Love, Luck and Aeroplanes."*

Brun, Tom, "The Indoor Tennis Court and Miss Lyra Brown Nickerson", *Senior Tennis 2008*, pp. 3-7.

Chroniclingamerica.loc.gov.

Cutter, William Roland ed. *American Biography, A New Cyclopedia, Vol.6, pp. 232*, New York, Lewis Historical Society Publishing Co. 1919.

Cutter, William Roland ed. *New England Families, genealogical and memorial. Vol. 3, p. 1122* New York, Lewis Historical Society Publishing Co. 1914.

Evans, Conway, *An Account Of Our Arresting Experiences*, Privately Printed 1914, Merrymount Press, Boston.

FamilySearch.com.

Findagrave.com.

Freeman, John R., *Improved Highway and Parkways, etc. for the East Side of Providence*, Loose Leaf Mfg. Co. City Printers, May 10, 1912.

Fuoco, Joe; *Rhode Island Mill Villages,* Arcadia Press, 1997

Google News Archive.

Huntsville Times, "Birmingham Woman Gets $25,000 Little Girl, $5000", Sept 11, 1916.

Miner, George Leland; *Angell's Lane, The History of a Little Street in Providence,* Akerman-Standard Press, 1948.

Lawless, Debra, *The Strange Death of Lyra Nickerson,* Nickerson Family Association Newsletter, Summer 2024.

Laxton, Glenn; *Hidden History of Rhode Island,* History Press Charleston, SC.

Newspapers.com.

Nickerson Family Association, Inc., www.nickersonassoc.org.

Providence Preservation Society, Mary A. Gowdy Library of House Histories, 63 Angell St.

Raben, Jonathan D., *Italian Americans and Federal Hill,* SEVENFISHESPRODUCTIONS, LLC, 2006.

The Providence Journal, "Lyra Brown Nickerson and two other individuals arrested and held as Russian spies", by German authorities in Europe. August 19, 1914.

The Providence Journal, "Tennis Ball" gala at the Indoor Tennis Court. November 1, 1914 "Society" section.

The Providence Daily Journal, "Lyra Brown Nickerson's death notice." August 31, 1916..

Providence Public Library Digital Collections/Cady Scrapbooks.

Reed, Senator Jack; *www.senate.reed.gov.*

Rhode Island Historical Society, Manuscripts Division, Nickerson House Records, 1884-2001, Cat. MSS 1122, Rick Stratton, July 2003.

Rhode Island School of Design (RISD).

U.S. Passport Applications.

Woodward, William McKensie, *Guide to Providence Architecture,* E. A. Johnson Co.,2003.

Acknowledgments

First and foremost, my wife Dacia told me of Lyra and the story of the Nickerson House. Dacia has encouraged me to investigate and document the sparkling facets of Lyra's life.

My interest in Nickerson history was also fostered by growing up with the seven other children of Roland and Lillian Nickerson. Thank you to Norma, Lucille (Lou), Wes and to the memory of Bob, Kathy, Elaine and Nancy.

My sister Lou's husband, Dale Anthony, provided valuable information and references regarding Edward I. Nickerson and the Joseph Rogers Brown family.

Cape Cod's Nickerson Family Association, myheritage.com, familysearch.com, newspapers.com and Tom Brun's article in the 2008 issue of Senior Tennis have been valuable resources for my research.

I extend my gratitude to Angelina Chute for her meticulous review of an early draft of this book.

I am also grateful to the following people who also reviewed drafts of this book: Tom and Matt Nickerson, Elissa Della Piana and Dacia herself.

About the Author

The author, Clive Lester Nickerson, the 7th of 8 children, was born in Brewer, Maine in 1941 and grew up in Bangor. An Engineering Physics graduate of the University of Maine, Clive had a long career as a Department of Defense engineer and scientist and was the Science Advisor to the Commanding General of XIII Airborne Corps and Fort Bragg.[94]

Lyra Brown Nickerson was born in Providence, Rhode Island in 1885. Both Clive and Lyra are descendants of the original English Settler of Chatham, Massachusetts on Cape Cod, William Nickerson. Clive's relationship to Lyra relative to William is 7th cousin once removed. Clive's lineage of the Nickerson family tree branched off to Maine with Reuben Nickerson II, who moved from Eastham, MA to Frankfort, ME in 1799. Lyra's line branched off to Rhode Island when Mulford Nickerson moved from Eastham, MA to Pawtucket, RI in 1821. Coincidentally, Reuben's wife, Lois Sparrow, and Mulford's wife, Esther Howes, had a common ancestor-Jonathan Sparrow, the son of English immigrant Capt. Jonathan Sparrow making Lyra and Clive's relationship even closer-6th cousin once removed. (See Appendix A: Family Ties)

Clive's interest in Lyra was sparked by the story his wife related to him about her experience as Dacia Libutti at the "Nickerson House" in Providence where she was inspired by the photograph of Lyra, the House's benefactor. The inspiration for this book resulted in subsequent research that documented the impact that Lyra's short life had on the city of Providence and just how remarkable the woman of Dacia's recollection had been.

---

[94] Photograph by Wes Nickerson.

www.ingramcontent.com/pod-product-compliance
Lightning Source LLC
Chambersburg PA
CBHW060209050426
42446CB00013B/3036